4-2-86

To Dorothy

Because you love whales
and we love you!

Tony + Patricia

Bonnie

Michael + Daniel

THE WORLD'S WHALES

A Pacific white-sided dolphin heads for the surface.

THE
WORLD'S WHALES
THE COMPLETE ILLUSTRATED GUIDE

STANLEY M. MINASIAN · KENNETH C. BALCOMB, III · LARRY FOSTER

SMITHSONIAN BOOKS
Washington, D.C.

Distributed by W. W. Norton & Company   New York, London

The Smithsonian Institution
Secretary S. Dillon Ripley
Director Office of Public Service
Ralph C. Rinzler
Director Smithsonian Institution Press
Felix C. Lowe

Smithsonian Books
Director Glen B. Ruh
Senior Editor Alexis Doster III
Editors Joe Goodwin, Patricia Gallagher
Assistant Editors Amy Donovan,
Eileen McWilliam, John F. Ross
Senior Picture Editor Nancy Strader
Picture Editors Patricia Upchurch,
Frances C. Rowsell
Picture Assistant R. Jenny Takacs
Copy Editor Dee McRae
Production Consultant Irv Garfield
Production Assistant June G. Armstrong
Business Manager Stephen J. Bergstrom
Office Assistant Susan Ozbey
Marketing Manager Margaret Kei Mooney
Marketing Assistant Melanie Levenson
Marketing Consultant William H. Kelty

Design Tom Suzuki
Mechanical Preparation Kenneth E. Hancock,
Peter Simmons, Jane Welihozkiy
Separation Lehigh Electronic Color
Typography Mid-Atlantic Photo Composition, Inc.
Printing W.A. Krueger Company

Manufactured in the United States of America

First Edition
5 4 3 2

Library of Congress Cataloging in Publication Data
Minasian, Stanley M., 1947
  The world's whales.

  Bibliography: p.
  Includes index.
  I. Cetacea. I. Balcomb, Kenneth C., 1940-
II. Foster, Larry A., 1934-   . III. Title.
QL737.C4M66 1984   599.5   84-14142
ISBN 0-89599-014-8

ACKNOWLEDGEMENTS

We wish to thank the following people,
without whose assistance this book might
never have become reality: Stephen
Leatherwood, Robert Pitman, John
McCosker, Keith Howell, George Lindsay,
and Birgit Winning. We also wish to thank
the following people for their contributions;
without which the book would have suffered
in quality: Don Reed, Thomas Grooms,
Sylvia Earle, Al Giddings, Roger Payne,
Grant R. Abel, P. Arnantho, Alan Baker,
Howard Garrett, Ken Minasian, Jake Page,
Marilyn Stansfield, Dale Rice, Felix Lowe,
Jackie Schonwald, Richard Sears, Fred
Wenzel, J. Michael Williamson, John
Dziadecki, Masaharu Nishiwaki, Harold Ross,
James Mead, Robbins Barstow, David
Withrow, Gerard Wellington, Frank Robson,
Stephen Spotte, David K. Caldwell, William
Dawbin, Irene and Heinrich Schatz, Gary
Robinson, Ron Kastelein, Roy Manstan,
Thomas Dohl, Isidore Szczepaniak, Marc
Webber, Masami Furuta, Randall Wells,
Bernie Tershy, Deborah and Mark Ferrari, Lee
Tepley, Ed Shallenberger, Peter Beamish,
Chen Pei-xun, Bill Rossiter, Michael Graybill,
Lloyd Parker, Jen and Des Bartlett, Lou Silva,
Jon Stern, Pieter Folkens, and all of the
photographers whose works we are privileged
to use in this project.

  Supporting organizations and institutions
include the Marine Mammal Fund, California
Academy of Sciences, Animal Welfare
Institute, Animal Protection Institute,
International Fund for Animal Welfare, and
the National Audubon Society. Also the
National Wildlife Federation, Defenders of
Wildlife, Greenpeace, Oceanic Society, Fund
for Animals, Cousteau Society, Mingen Island
Cetacean Study, Ocean Research and
Education Society, General Whale, and the
Center for Environmental Education/Whale
Protection Fund.

This book is dedicated
to the memory of
WILSON AYERS CLARK

CONTENTS

Stephen Leatherwood

A Commerson's dolphin leaps into the air.

FOREWORD

The Smithsonian Institution has given us many instructive yet evocative books which bring to life some little-known species or cultures with which we share the planet. It has just done it again, this time giving us a book which manages to convey the wonder and grace of some of our strangest and largest fellow inhabitants, the whale, dolphins, and porpoises—the cetaceans.

Given the rapidly increasing interest in cetaceans, this book fills an important niche and deserves a place among the handful of recent books on cetaceans that are really worth owning. Its authors, Ken Balcomb and Stan Minasian, have spent between them an exceptional amount of time at sea watching whales, dolphins, and porpoises. The illustrator, Larry Foster, has a well-deserved reputation as the artist who takes most care in making his illustrations of whales accurate. He is indefatigable about running down unpublished photographs of obscure species taken by little-known photographers in remote places, with the result that he has assembled an extraordinary reference collection of whale photographs (the very thing that keeps his illustrations so honest). This book makes available for the first time a similar kind of collection—one assembled by author Stan Minasian over an 11-year period. It is a portfolio of over 160 photographs (most in color) illustrating almost all cetacean species. Of greatest interest: *all* these pictures are of live animals and all but a few are of animals that were swimming free in the open sea when they were photographed.

Were the book only offering this portfolio of photographs it would be worth owning. Photographic collections like this haven't been published before and this one is going to open a lot of eyes. But this is not just a picture book: there are chapters on every major subdivision of whales that include write-ups of each species, in addition to a delightful introductory chapter reviewing the origin, evolution, feeding habits, senses, diving abilities, communication, and mating of cetaceans. I found this chapter to be a most engaging treatment of the subject, and would recommend it to anyone who has been bitten by curiosity about these most elusive of mammals and who would like to know more. (In fact, treatments as nice as this don't come along very often.)

If you have a relative or an acquaintance young or old who has been somewhat bitten by a fascination for whales but whose interest is still only vaguely formed, give them this book and then watch what happens. They'll be launched—permanently—and you will have provided just the right lift. Considering that we live in a world so entirely different from the world in which whales dwell, and that most of us never see them at all; and considering that everything surrounding their lives is shrouded in almost complete ignorance, it is a little hard to understand just where an interest in whales arises. Well, all we need to know is that it does arise. And once it has arisen it is nice to have ways to make it stronger and more lasting. In their introductory chapter the authors note that it is toward a greater knowledge and hope for the survival of whales that the effort of writing this book was devoted. They succeed admirably.

Whales have recently become a symbol of the wild world. It has been absolutely fascinating to me to watch it happen. They tend to lodge in the hearts of people—sometimes they lodge crosswise where they stick for life. Books like this one can help to promote that kind of terminal affliction. May the disease sweep over all humankind—the whaling nations included.

—Roger Payne

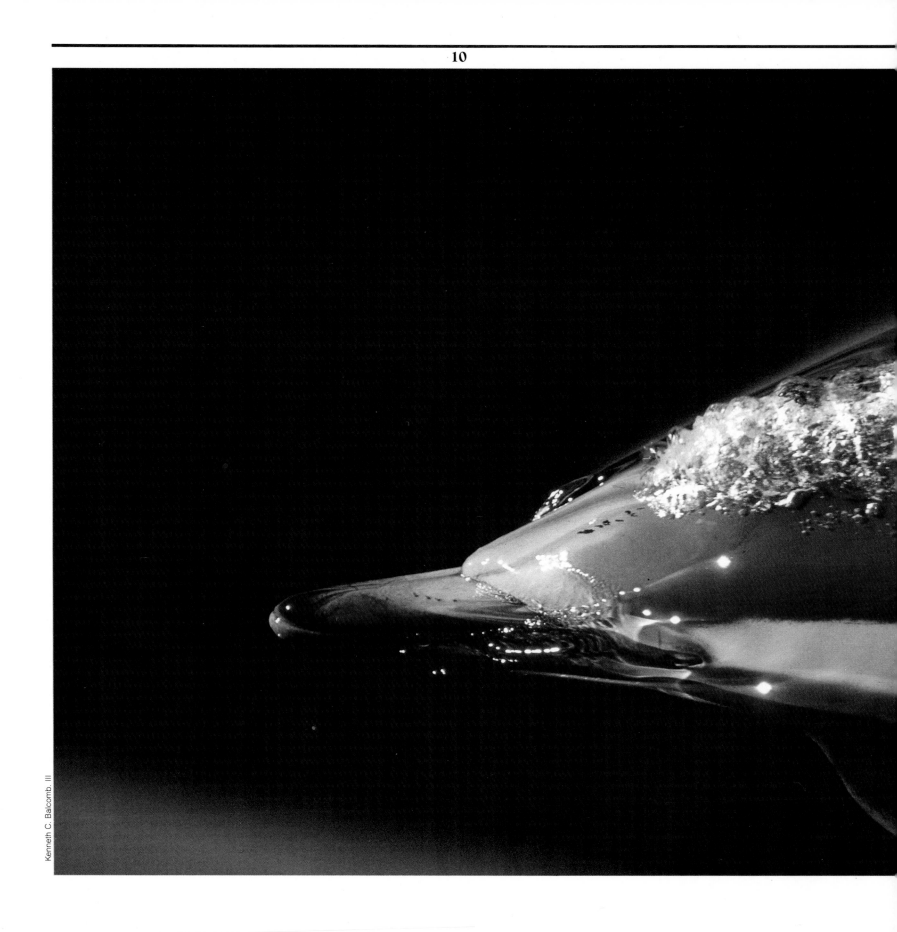

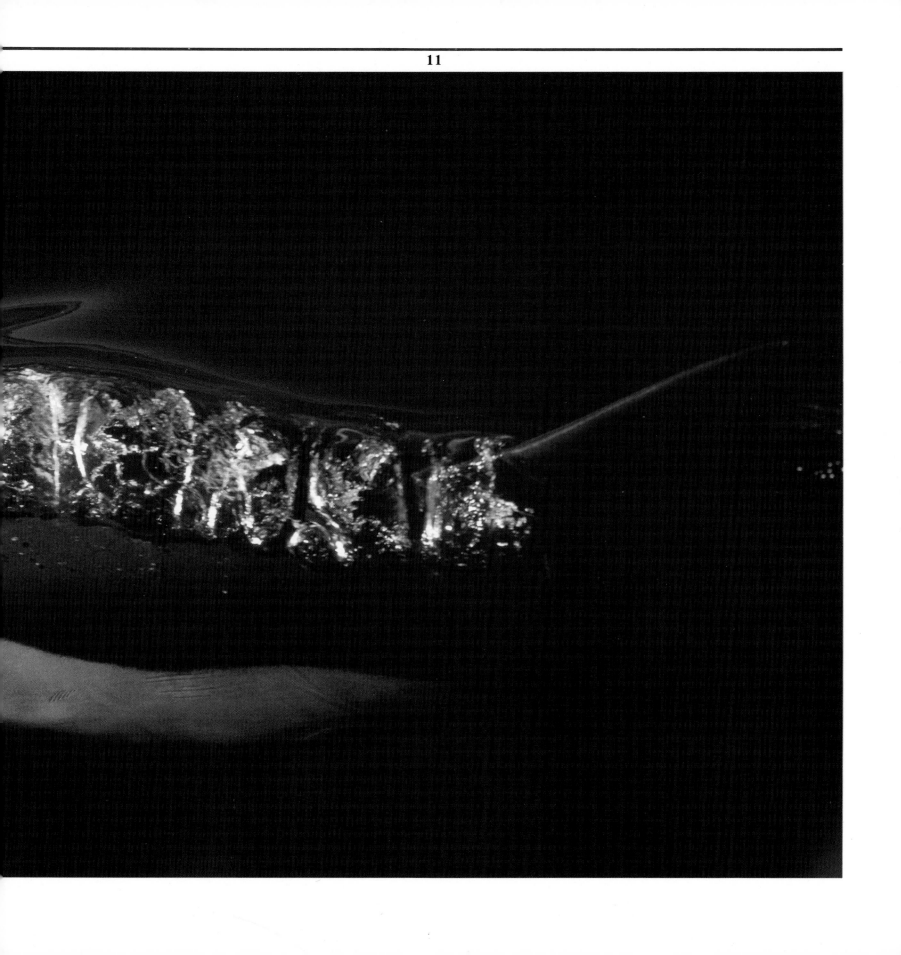

Pages 10-11: A common dolphin at the surface expels a breath; 12-13: Humpback whale just below the surface; 14-15: Killer whales at the surface.

David Rugh, NMFS

Aerial photograph of a gray whale surfacing.

THE TAXONOMY OF WHALES

Cetaceans—whales, dolphins, and porpoises—have been categorized taxonomically according to the Linnaean system developed by the Swedish botanist, Carolus Linnaeus (1707-1778). Within the animal kingdom, cetaceans belong to the phylum Chordata, because they have notochords (precursors of the spinal chord), to the subphylum Vertebrata since they have backbones, to the class Mammalia since they suckle their young from their mammaries, and to the order Cetacea since they are carnivorous and wholly aquatic. Within the order Cetacea, two clear suborders emerge—Odontoceti (toothed whales) and Mysticeti (baleen whales). From there, anatomical and behavioral features determine more specific classifications of family, genus, and species.

In each species description, a name and date follow the Linnaean classification. The name and date indicate the individual who first described the animal and the year of discovery. Parentheses around the name and date indicate a change in the genus name to a more accurate taxonomic category sometime after the first description.

ARTIST'S NOTE

The authors of *The World's Whales* used photographs of living cetaceans whenever possible. For those species which had been described from life but never photographed, paintings were prepared, keeping as close to the photograpic ideal of the book as possible. Photographs of close relatives of the unphotographed species were selected and used as a base; new colors and body conformations were painted over the photograph. In this way, good representational accuracy could be achieved, and the paintings blended harmoniously with the photographs in the book.

A Bryde's whale calf feeds on its side.

WHALES, DOLPHINS, AND PORPOISES

Illustrations for *The World's Whales* are by Larry Foster.

SOME TIME between 70 million and 50 million years ago, after the last of the dinosaurs had died and mammals had inherited the land, one or more groups of mammals waded back into the water, presumably to feed on the abundant plant and animal forms there. These pig-sized, four-legged, warm-blooded, placental creatures adapted quickly to their new habitat and soon gave rise to a new branch in the evolutionary tree—the order Cetacea, which today includes all of the world's whales, dolphins, and porpoises. Later, several other great mammalian surges to the sea led to the evolution of the seals, sea lions, and sea cows we know today, but none of these is related directly to the Cetacea.

Three groups of cetaceans arose from the land-dwelling ancestor or ancestors. The earliest group, the Archaeoceti, or ancient whales, died out about 20 million years ago. Of the two surviving groups, one, the Odontoceti or toothed whales, evolved specialized teeth to grasp fish and other relatively large prey such as squid, while the other living group, the Mysticeti, or baleen whales, lost their teeth and developed very large mouths equipped with filtering fringes or baleen with which they trap large numbers of very small organisms. Both of these evolutionary paths proved to be successful, and each group has diversified to fill various niches. Although the demands of mobility, heat conservation, and sensory awareness in an aquatic environment have caused both groups to evolve superficially similar body forms, they are really quite different animals.

It is not yet clear whether today's whales have a common ancestor. However, a currently favored theory holds that both primitive baleen whales and toothed whales derived from the archaeocetes, and they, in turn, had probably evolved millions of years earlier in the Paleocene or Lower Miocene epoch from a group of small, generalized, carnivorous land mammals called creodonts. The earliest and most primitive cetacean fossil yet found, *Pakicetus inachus*, dates from the early

EVOLUTION OF WHALES

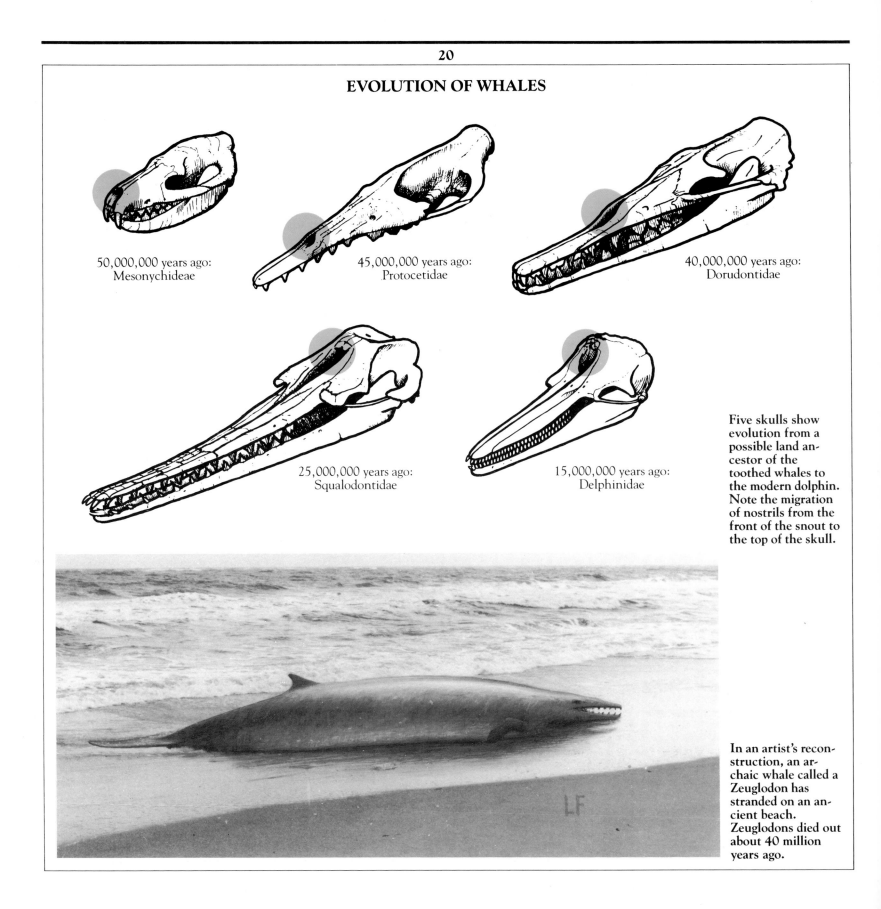

50,000,000 years ago:
Mesonychideae

45,000,000 years ago:
Protocetidae

40,000,000 years ago:
Dorudontidae

25,000,000 years ago:
Squalodontidae

15,000,000 years ago:
Delphinidae

Five skulls show evolution from a possible land ancestor of the toothed whales to the modern dolphin. Note the migration of nostrils from the front of the snout to the top of the skull.

In an artist's reconstruction, an archaic whale called a Zeuglodon has stranded on an ancient beach. Zeuglodons died out about 40 million years ago.

Eocene epoch (about 60 million years ago) of Pakistan; it seems to have been an amphibious creature preying on fish in the shallow waters of the ancient eastern Tethys Sea.

The Odontoceti, or toothed whales (from the Greek: *odontos*—tooth; *ketos*—whale), comprising 66 generally recognized species, include dolphins and porpoises as well as the giant sperm whale of *Moby Dick* fame and other whales of intermediate size. All of these whales are characterized by one external nostril, or blowhole, as well as teeth. Toothed whales typically use their teeth to seize prey such as squid, shrimp, fish, or other creatures which are then swallowed whole. (With few exceptions, whales generally do not tear apart or chew their food.)

Among the toothed whales, several families—closely related groups of species—have evolved, each with distinct patterns of behavior and geographic distribution. Each of these families will be discussed at greater length in the chapters following this introduction, but briefly they are:

- Physeteridae: Large, deep-diving, gregarious sperm whales—and dwarf and pygmy sperm whales—with a protruding forehead and numerous conical teeth which erupt and are functional in the lower jaw only.

- Ziphiidae: Medium-sized, deep-diving whales whose snouts are elongated, giving them a "beaked" appearance—having, with one exception, a few peglike teeth (usually two) which erupt in the lower jaw only and are apparently not functional in feeding. The exception, Shepherd's beaked whale, has numerous small, conical teeth in addition to two large teeth which erupt in males.

- Delphinidae: True dolphins, small to medium-sized, including some called "whales" with many functional interlocking conical teeth in upper and lower jaw. These dolphins are adapted to marine habitats.

- Monodontidae: Medium-sized whales with relatively few teeth, generally nonfunctional in feeding. There are only two species, both adapted to Arctic marine waters. In one of these, the narwhal, a single tooth is highly specialized to form a long spiraled tusk.

- Platanistidae: Small dolphins with a long, slender snout—with many functional interlocking, conical teeth in upper and lower jaws. For the most part, these dolphins have become adapted to freshwater and estuarine habitats.

- Phocoenidae: Porpoises with an inflexible neck and small, spade-shaped teeth. Their distribution is entirely marine with a tendency toward inshore rather than pelagic (offshore) waters.

In their habits, the toothed whales have developed along three principal lines of distribution and prey selection. Some are oceanic deep divers which feed upon bottom-dwelling species; others are oceanic but feed on prey species living at or near the surface of the sea, while still others occupy the productive inshore habitats. The first group includes the giant sperm whale, which is capable of hour-long dives at depths exceeding 1.5 kilometers (one mile), and the two smaller species of sperm whale; the Ziphiidae, or beaked whales, which are generally found in areas of water depths greater than 1.5 kilometers (one mile), particularly near the edges of major ocean currents and deep sea escarpments; and some species of Delphinidae, notably in the genera *Globicephala* and *Grampus*. These oceanic creatures occasionally venture into shallow waters in their search for prey, and they may drift inshore with ocean currents, but they are maladapted to cope with shallows and shorelines and may become disoriented and strand themselves.

The oceanic near-surface feeders are characterized by the dolphins such as those in the genera *Stenella*, *Delphinus*, and *Lagenorhynchus* These are gregarious animals which often travel in herds of up to several thousand individuals. Their distribution is worldwide in temperate and tropical seas, with *Delphinus* venturing in large numbers into the Mediterranean Sea, the Black Sea, and the Gulf of California. These oceanic near-surface feeders generally eat squid and fish associated with the deep scattering layers (DSL), often by night as the prey species rise to within the first hundred meters (330 feet) or so of the sea's surface.

Inshore feeders are represented by the bottlenose dolphin and the harbor porpoise which may be found as close inshore as the surf zone, as well as in many of the busiest harbors of the world. The smaller harbor porpoise is very shy and secretive in its habits, while the friendly and curious bottlenose dolphin frequently announces its presence by splashing and sporting in the bow-waves of vessels under way. These inshore species feed upon schooling fish, such as herring and mullet, and a great variety of invertebrates and near-bottom species.

In addition to these offshore/inshore and deep-water/shallow-water distinctions, whole species' distribution patterns may be dictated by water temperature, most probably as temperature determines the distribution of less mobile prey species. While the vast majority of the toothed whales inhabit the world's temperate seas—perhaps moving slightly toward colder regions to feed and warmer ones to breed—a few toothed whales have adapted entirely to freezing arctic waters, some others to warm tropical seas.

Wherever they may live and feed, all toothed whales share a sonarlike ability to examine their surroundings and find prey by echolocation. While most terrestrial mammals depend largely on vision for

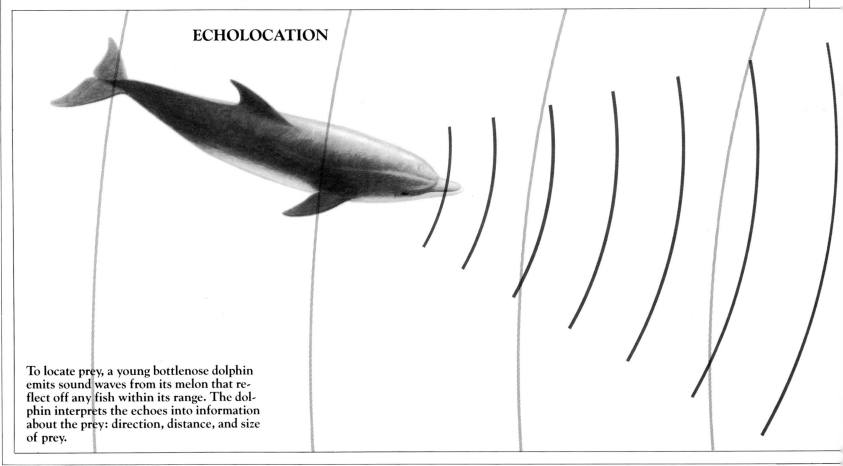

ECHOLOCATION

To locate prey, a young bottlenose dolphin emits sound waves from its melon that reflect off any fish within its range. The dolphin interprets the echoes into information about the prey: direction, distance, and size of prey.

awareness of their environments, marine mammals live with a scarcity of light. The whales' ancestors, who probably saw quite well in air, necessarily adapted to the poor visibility typical of underwater environments.

Hearing, however, is not impaired underwater as sight is. On the contrary, it is enhanced because water transmits the pressure waves of sound much more rapidly and effectively than does air, even for extreme distances and depths. Accordingly, the toothed whales, like bats, have developed means by which they emit special sounds that travel out from their heads and reflect off objects around them, producing echoes they can hear and interpret. In this fashion they locate objects, including prey, in their vicinity, and perceive instantaneously the range, bearing, and configuration of each. Some dolphins, tested in aquarium conditions, were able to distinguish a fish they liked to eat from one they did not, solely by echolocation, even though the two fish were identical in size and shape. Presumably, the dolphins determined the texture or internal structure of the two fish by echolocation. In other tests, dolphins have been able to distinguish between objects the approximate size of a B-B shot and a kernel of corn at a distance equivalent to 50 paces. Their acoustic discrimination is superb! At ease with their acoustic abilities, blind or blindfolded dolphins will move about freely and feed normally, but a deaf or deafened dolphin will become frightened, disoriented, and reluctant to move.

We humans usually consider that only we can think conceptually and make use of sophisticated linguistic constructs for communication. Animal communication, if we assume that animals can communicate at all, generally is believed to be inferior. Our assumption

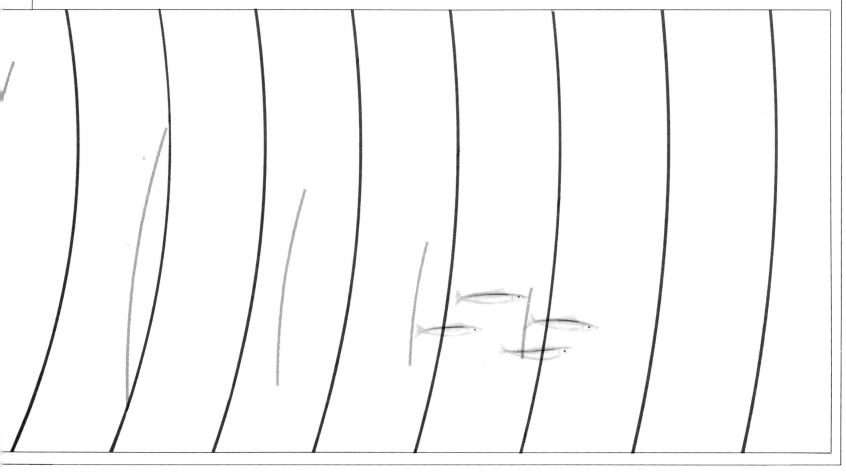

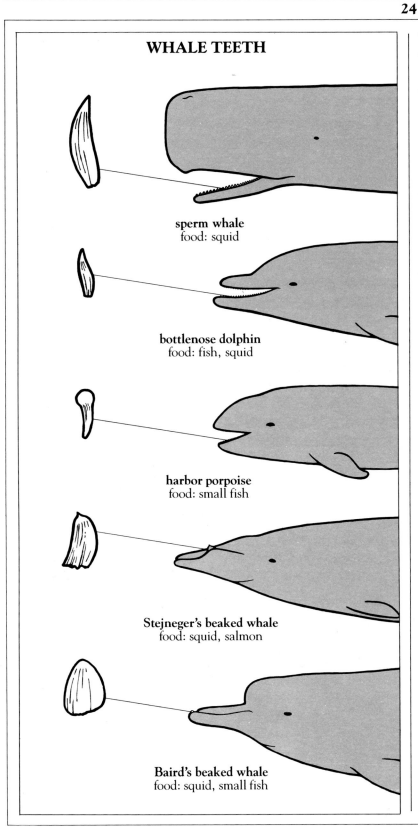

WHALE TEETH

sperm whale
food: squid

bottlenose dolphin
food: fish, squid

harbor porpoise
food: small fish

Stejneger's beaked whale
food: squid, salmon

Baird's beaked whale
food: squid, small fish

of superiority in this regard may be unwarranted. In addition to finding food and resolving exquisite detail in their surroundings by echolocating, many toothed whales have obviously developed the ability to communicate with one another using whistles, clicks, and calls of various sorts. No one really knows yet if they "say" anything, much less whether they are capable of abstract thinking. It is certain, however, that they do communicate, and they often coordinate very complex group activities by such communication.

Nevertheless, sophisticated acoustic skills, ability to communicate, and a large and well-developed brain do not prove that cetacean intelligence is equal or superior to that of human beings as some investigators have suggested. Both humans and cetaceans have evolved in different ways, adapting to very different conditions, and it is we who define intelligence in such a way as to exclude other animals. Marvelous cetacean "intelligence" may one day be proven, but that will not be until we can understand their communications. Until then we must be patient. Modern explorations into interspecies communication have just begun and the results of such explorations must be evaluated carefully. After all, human beings have developed a sonar capability through the use of machines only in the past few decades, while odontocetes have been refining their acoustic apparatus for about 50 million years. It should come as no surprise that they are spectacularly proficient with it—more so than we by far.

Beyond echolocation, the ancestors of the odontocetes needed other adaptations to be successful in the marine environment. They needed mobility and agility in the water, and the capacity to make long, deep dives. The earliest cetaceans quickly became streamlined, losing their drag-producing hair and evolving a spindle-shaped body. To stay warm, they developed a blubber layer and improved their circulatory thermoregulation mechanisms. They also developed great sensitivity and control over their entire skin and their appendages, which evolved from legs, paws, and tails into paddle-shaped fins and flukes. Their nostrils migrated from the front of the face to the top of the head, where breathing could be accomplished with little or no hindrance to forward movement. And their respiratory physiology and internal anatomy changed, ultimately making possible—for some species, at least—dives of astonishing depth and duration.

An adaptation no less successful than that of the toothed whales was accomplished by the second major group of cetaceans, the Mysticeti (from the Greek: *mystax*—moustache; *ketos*—whale). Instead of seizing one or two moderate-sized prey at a time, the Mysticeti, or baleen whales, consume enormous numbers of very small prey with every mouthful. The tremendous blooms of invertebrate organisms and small schooling fish that occur seasonally in various regions of the seas provide an ideal albeit episodic food supply for those creatures that can get to them first and eat the most. In response to these blooms, baleen whale evolution has been characterized by migrations to and from the feeding grounds—often journeys of thousands of miles—and the development of sievelike food-gathering structures—baleen plates—in place of teeth. These baleen plates or baleens are akin to the epidermal ridges on the roof of the human mouth but have a texture somewhat similar to fingernail tissue, and they grow to considerable lengths—sometimes several feet. While the actual number of baleen plates in the mouth varies from one species to another, and one individual to another, ordinarily there are several hundred. Each is tapered with a bristly fringe facing inward, and a straight slatlike edge facing outward. The plates are spaced a little less than a centimeter—a quarter of an inch—apart (the precise spacing also varies from species to species and individual to individual) with the result that the complete set of baleen plates somewhat resembles a palm frond attached along its entire length to the whale's upper gum. In addition to baleen plates,

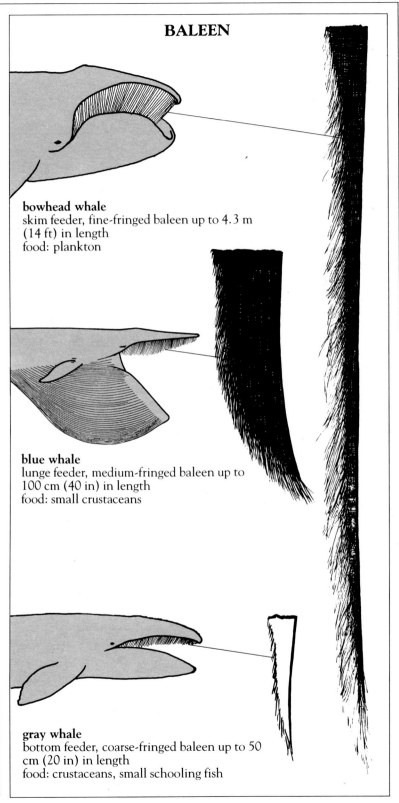

BALEEN

bowhead whale
skim feeder, fine-fringed baleen up to 4.3 m (14 ft) in length
food: plankton

blue whale
lunge feeder, medium-fringed baleen up to 100 cm (40 in) in length
food: small crustaceans

gray whale
bottom feeder, coarse-fringed baleen up to 50 cm (20 in) in length
food: crustaceans, small schooling fish

COMPARATIVE SIZES OF WHALES, DOLPHINS, AND PORPOISES

Sizes represent the average approximate length of cetaceans found today.

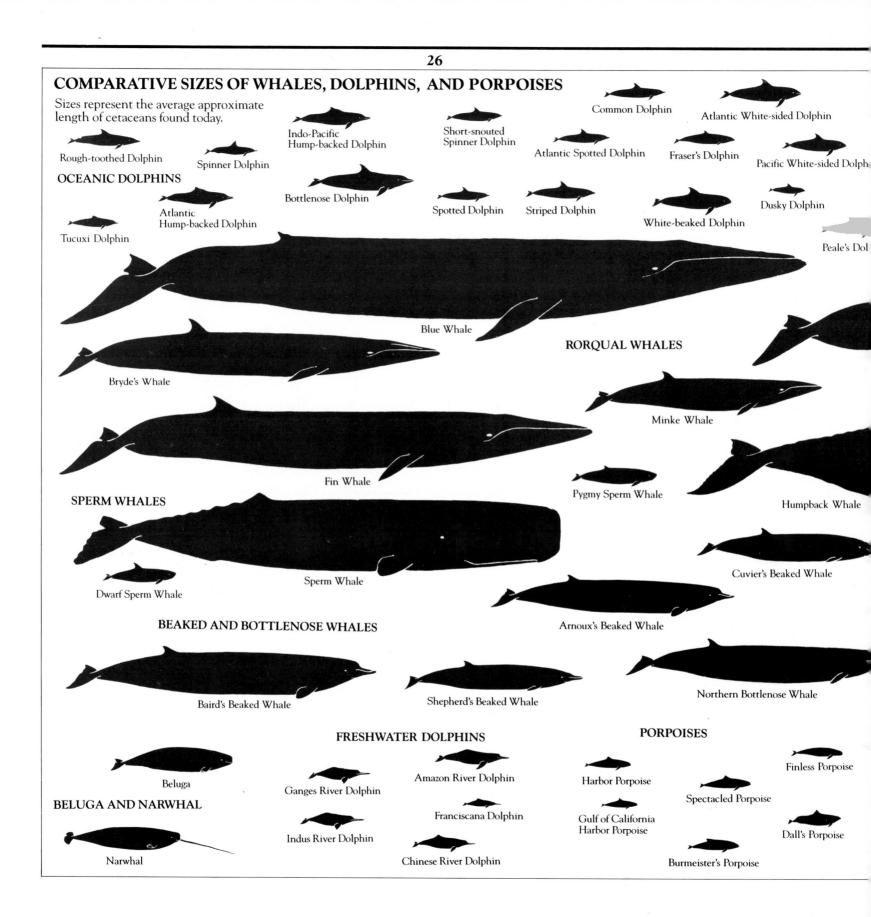

OCEANIC DOLPHINS

Rough-toothed Dolphin

Spinner Dolphin

Indo-Pacific Hump-backed Dolphin

Short-snouted Spinner Dolphin

Common Dolphin

Atlantic White-sided Dolphin

Atlantic Spotted Dolphin

Fraser's Dolphin

Pacific White-sided Dolphin

Bottlenose Dolphin

Spotted Dolphin

Striped Dolphin

White-beaked Dolphin

Dusky Dolphin

Tucuxi Dolphin

Atlantic Hump-backed Dolphin

Peale's Dolphin

Blue Whale

RORQUAL WHALES

Bryde's Whale

Minke Whale

Fin Whale

Pygmy Sperm Whale

Humpback Whale

SPERM WHALES

Sperm Whale

Cuvier's Beaked Whale

Dwarf Sperm Whale

Arnoux's Beaked Whale

BEAKED AND BOTTLENOSE WHALES

Northern Bottlenose Whale

Baird's Beaked Whale

Shepherd's Beaked Whale

FRESHWATER DOLPHINS

PORPOISES

Beluga

Amazon River Dolphin

Harbor Porpoise

Finless Porpoise

BELUGA AND NARWHAL

Ganges River Dolphin

Spectacled Porpoise

Franciscana Dolphin

Gulf of California Harbor Porpoise

Indus River Dolphin

Dall's Porpoise

Narwhal

Chinese River Dolphin

Burmeister's Porpoise

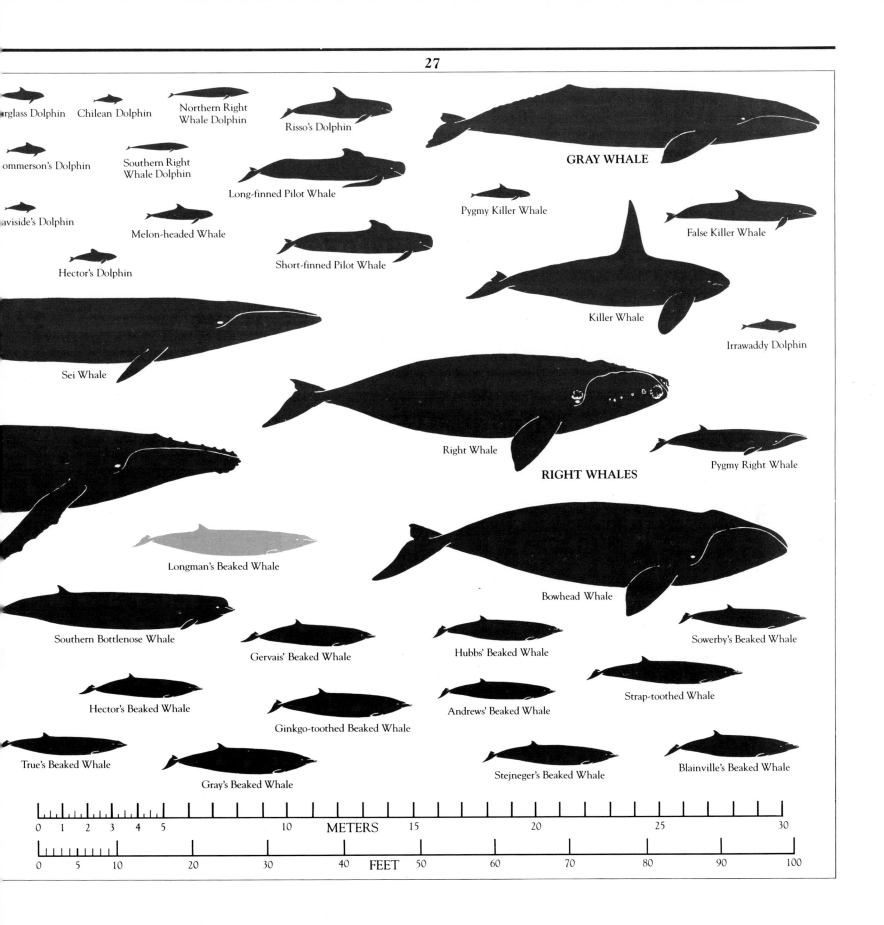

Hourglass Dolphin

Chilean Dolphin

Northern Right Whale Dolphin

Risso's Dolphin

Commerson's Dolphin

Southern Right Whale Dolphin

Long-finned Pilot Whale

GRAY WHALE

Pygmy Killer Whale

False Killer Whale

Haviside's Dolphin

Melon-headed Whale

Short-finned Pilot Whale

Killer Whale

Hector's Dolphin

Irrawaddy Dolphin

Sei Whale

Right Whale

RIGHT WHALES

Pygmy Right Whale

Longman's Beaked Whale

Bowhead Whale

Southern Bottlenose Whale

Gervais' Beaked Whale

Hubbs' Beaked Whale

Sowerby's Beaked Whale

Hector's Beaked Whale

Ginkgo-toothed Beaked Whale

Andrews' Beaked Whale

Strap-toothed Whale

True's Beaked Whale

Gray's Beaked Whale

Stejneger's Beaked Whale

Blainville's Beaked Whale

0 1 2 3 4 5 10 METERS 15 20 25 30

0 5 10 20 30 40 FEET 50 60 70 80 90 100

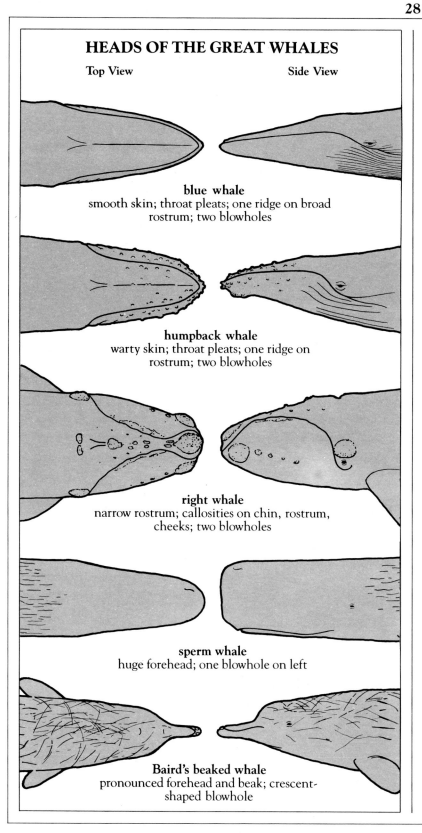

HEADS OF THE GREAT WHALES

Top View   **Side View**

blue whale
smooth skin; throat pleats; one ridge on broad
rostrum; two blowholes

humpback whale
warty skin; throat pleats; one ridge on
rostrum; two blowholes

right whale
narrow rostrum; callosities on chin, rostrum,
cheeks; two blowholes

sperm whale
huge forehead; one blowhole on left

Baird's beaked whale
pronounced forehead and beak; crescent-
shaped blowhole

these whales are characterized by two external nostrils, or blowholes.

The manner in which baleen whales feed varies with the species of whale and prey, and sometimes with individual style. All, however, dine very efficiently on the small organisms near the lower levels of the food chain. The various species of baleen whales have become specialized according to the habitats and habits of their prey. Some, such as the right whales, have very finely fringed baleen, with which they can filter and consume very small planktonic organisms simply by skimming open mouthed through the water. In this manner a right whale can filter thousands of cubic meters of sea water and extract from it approximately 1,700 kilograms (two tons) of nearly microscopic plankton per day.

Other whales, such as the fin and the blue, have more coarsely fringed baleen, and feed upon correspondingly larger, often active prey that swarm in dense schools. To catch the shrimplike crustaceans and small schooling fish that are staple items in their diets, these whales must swim rapidly and with enough agility to herd a school into a tight mass, and then grab as many individuals as possible with a single, lunging gulp. These whales have longitudinal pleats of skin extending from the chin to the chest or belly region making the whale's throat enormously expandable, like a pelican's throat pouch. A large whale's distensible throat permits it to trap thousands of gallons of food and water with each mouthful. The whale's belly and jaw muscles then contract to force the water out between the baleen plates, leaving bushels of tiny prey in the whale's mouth. In this way the largest species may filter many thousands of cubic meters of water and consume about 3,600 kilograms (four tons) of food per day.

The gray whale employs a feeding style that differs from that of any other whale. The gray is the most "primitive" of all whales in appearance, and its feeding habits are presumably similar to those of the ancestors of all baleen whales. Gray whales typically feed on small fish and invertebrates found in or near the bottom sediments in shallow waters. Some observations have been made which suggest that the whale's tongue acts as a hydraulic piston in the mouth. Apparently, the whale swims on its side near the ocean floor and pushes water out of its mouth through its baleen plates and lower gums, stirring up the bottom sediment. Then as it draws its tongue back, the sediment and the organisms living in or near it are drawn into its mouth. As the whale rises to the surface, it may sluice its mouth with clean water and swallow its catch, sometimes gaining a gravity assist by sticking its head vertically out of the water. The sluicing portion of the maneuver may be omitted in order to suck creatures from the bottom. This method of feeding on bottom species is popularly known as "grubbing." Evidence offered in support of this picture of the gray whale's feeding habits includes the fact that many gray whales taken by whaling have been found with rocks, sticks, seaweed, and a great variety of shallow-water, bottom-dwelling species in their stomachs. Also, there have been direct observations of suction feeding upon invertebrates by a young gray whale in captivity; and indirect evidence from troughlike depressions in bottom sediments where gray whales have been feeding.

Apparently, gray whales have little competition for their food supplies—this may have contributed to their recovering twice from near extinction due to whaling in the past century. Now they thrive again in the inshore waters of their ancestors.

The world's seas cover 71 percent of the planet's surface, or roughly 370 million square kilometers (140 million square miles). Their total volume is about 1.5 billion cubic kilometers (350 million cubic miles), their average depth 4 kilometers (2.5 miles). Most of the radiated energy that falls on the earth from the sun falls upon the sea, heating its surface waters and providing light for the photosynthetic organisms that

exist there at the primary level of a food chain leading up to the whales and other marine mammals. In the sea as on land, the changes of season affect the amount of food available in any particular region. Temperature differences between water masses in different parts of the sea create imbalances in the air and water resulting in the patterns of oceanic currents that dominate the weather both at sea and on land.

While the marine environment changes continually in some respects, it is very stable in others: as a swimming medium it provides continuous physical support; it resists rapid change in temperature; it is fairly uniformly saline; and it contains, dissolved within it, all the trace elements necessary to life as well as essential gasses such as oxygen and carbon dioxide.

Water weighs about one gram per cubic centimeter (62.4 pounds per cubic foot) and is virtually incompressible; the pressure on any organism in the water, therefore, increases with depth. Increased pressure presents little problem for fish and invertebrates such as squid, or for plants, which have no air sacs within them. But for a whale, or for any other creature that takes air into its lungs at the surface, pressure becomes a critical factor that must be dealt with if the animal is to penetrate very far beneath the surface.

The air we breathe is composed of approximately 80 percent nitrogen and 20 percent oxygen, and atmospheric pressure at sea level is about 2,300 newtons per square meter (14.7 pounds per square inch). We know that human divers may suffer the bends (nitrogen bubbles forming in the blood and other body fluids) if they fail to ventilate and decompress adequately when returning from dives to depths at which the pressure is equal to as little as twice the atmospheric pressure at sea level—20 meters (64 feet). They may also suffer nitrogen narcosis, the condition known as "raptures of the deep," in which nitrogen in nerve membranes under pressure can lead to progressive disruption of central nervous system functions, followed by disorientation and unconsciousness. At depth, a single lungful of

A. Rus Hoezel, courtesy Jon Stern

A feeding minke whale breaches, throat pleats distended and water trailing from its mouth.

surface air contains enough nitrogen to bring on the effects of narcosis. The problem of raptures is compounded for divers using self-contained underwater breathing apparatus (SCUBA) gear: because the air itself is breathed under pressure, more molecules of nitrogen are taken in with each lungful. For this reason, divers working at depths greater than 50 meters (160 feet) often use a helium-oxygen mixture for breathing, rather than ordinary compressed air, because helium does not produce the rapturous effects.

The problems of pressure and nitrogen notwithstanding, some cetaceans are capable of prolonged dives to depths as great as 1,500 meters (a mile), where the pressure on their bodies exceeds 7.7 million newtons per square meter (2,600 pounds per square inch), or about 180 times the atmospheric pressure at sea level. Researchers are still investigating the methods by which whales have solved the problems inherent in mammalian diving. Although they have not yet answered the central questions, they have discovered many surprising adaptive features of these animals' anatomy and physiology.

For example, they have found that whales' lungs collapse at great depths, as would be expected, but their ribs do not break, as human ribs would, because the cetacean rib cage is less rigid than that of land mammals. They have found that whale blood has a high percentage of fats with an affinity for nitrogen that reduce the quantity of dissolved nitrogen available to nerve membranes in a whale's blood. It is even supposed that excess nitrogen in the airways may be eliminated with a phlegm of fat droplets in the expired air when a whale surfaces and "spouts." Those who have photographed whales can attest to the existence of this phlegm after particularly close encounters with whale breath, when they have had to wipe the oily mist from camera lenses.

To obtain enough oxygen to remain at depth for a long period, a whale fills its lungs to about 90 percent of their total capacity with each breath, compared with about 20 percent among terrestrial mammals. Although they do not have proportionately larger lungs than land mammals, whales do have more blood in proportion to their total body weight, and more hemoglobin (an oxygen-carrying substance) in their blood which allows more oxygen to be taken from each breath. Whale blood chemistry permits a more efficient net transfer of oxygen to tissue at any pressure than that of land mammals by being slightly more acidic. Aside from blood, whale muscle tissue is rich in myoglobin, a substance similar to hemoglobin in its oxygen-binding properties. Myoglobin stores oxygen in a whale's muscles, making it available for work on demand in the absence of an oxygenated blood supply. Additionally, whale body tissue easily adapts to anaerobic (without oxygen) metabolism for short periods of time, with the result that whales have a wider tolerance for the consequences of oxygen deprivation than do their counterparts on land.

In addition to being anatomically adapted to withstand great pressure, a marine mammal must maintain its body temperature in the chilling waters of the seas, where temperatures may be as much as 16° Celsius (60° Fahrenheit) lower than the animal's own temperature. To overcome this, all whales have developed an insulating layer of blubber (fat which may be a third of a meter, or a foot, or more thick), and have evolved the basic torpedo or spindle shape with small appendages to reduce the ratio of surface area to body volume (body heat is produced in proportion to body volume, but is dissipated in proportion to body surface area). Whales also have developed to an exquisite degree a counter-current heat exchange system of arteries and veins to and from their fins, flukes, and flippers. This system allows the warm arterial blood pulsing out from the whale's body core to relinquish its heat to a surrounding network of incoming veins in each appendage, so that heat loss to the surrounding water is greatly reduced. When a whale is overheated from exertion, for example, the effect of the system can be reversed, so that heat from the whale is given up to the water, thus cooling the animal.

Animal tissue is approximately the same density as sea water. Therefore, when the whales' ancestors returned to the sea, the water supported them so that they no longer needed the structural support of heavy bones and feet planted firmly on the ground. As the mammals adapted to their watery environment their bony structures became important principally as a frame for attachment of propulsive muscles: the vertebral column was compressed in the neck and chest area while it expanded toward the tail, providing effective leverage for the propelling flukes that swept up and down through the water; and the front legs evolved to

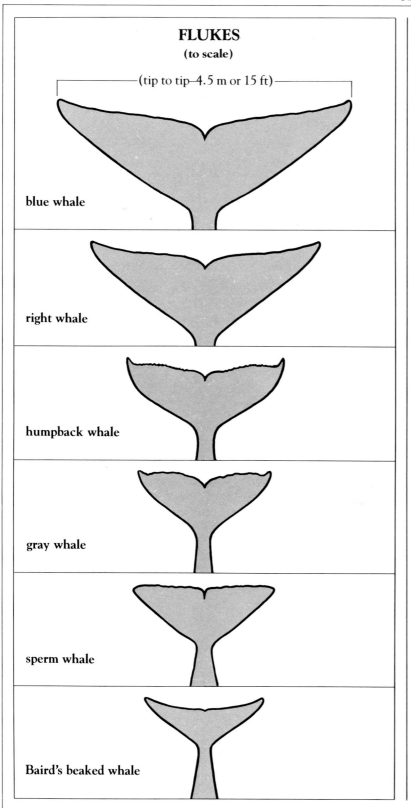

FLUKES
(to scale)

(tip to tip—4.5 m or 15 ft)

blue whale

right whale

humpback whale

gray whale

sperm whale

Baird's beaked whale

become paddles, or flippers, which controlled water flow and steering.

The supportive properties of water also freed whales from gravitational and structural restraints on their size, although, of course, not all became leviathans. A huge terrestrial mammal such as the elephant must support its ponderous weight on thick, stumpy legs, while the blue whale—heavier than 20 elephants—is buoyed easily and gracefully by the sea.

Although constrained by heredity and the efficiency of size in catching prey, a whale is not limited structurally to any size. In large measure, each species will evolve to a particular size in response to the food supplies available to its lineage, limiting its size. As the large whales evolved to feed efficiently upon large quantities of seasonally abundant swarms of small prey in the open sea, small whales and dolphins evolved to feed upon smaller numbers of larger, individual prey animals. The smallest porpoise can catch single fish efficiently in shallow inshore waters, where a large whale could not survive. Conversely, large whales can harvest the enormous seasonal zooplankton "crops" of the open sea more efficiently.

Along with the rest of the mammalian body, whale skin has evolved in response to its watery environment. As already mentioned, whales have lost virtually all of their drag-producing hair, and developed a smooth, rubbery skin which ripples elastically as water flows over it when the whale moves. These skin ripples produce a smooth, rather than turbulent, water flow along its surface. This unique ability permits a whale to attain far greater speeds than a comparably sized rigid structure might reach with equal propulsion power—a feature that has attracted the experimental interest of many naval architects.

All creatures must be able to locate others of their kind in order to reproduce. Many are gregarious, as well, living in groups to feed, for protection, perhaps

PARTS OF A WHALE

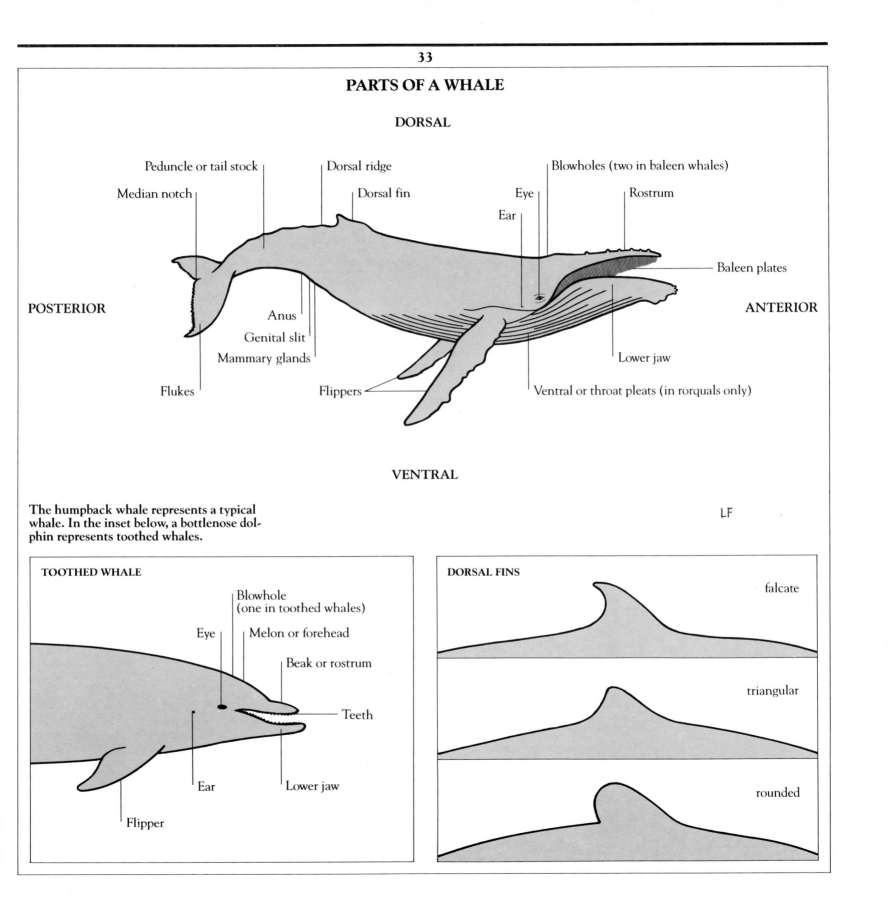

DORSAL

Peduncle or tail stock

Median notch

Dorsal ridge

Dorsal fin

Blowholes (two in baleen whales)

Eye

Ear

Rostrum

Baleen plates

POSTERIOR

ANTERIOR

Anus

Genital slit

Mammary glands

Lower jaw

Flukes

Flippers

Ventral or throat pleats (in rorquals only)

VENTRAL

The humpback whale represents a typical whale. In the inset below, a bottlenose dolphin represents toothed whales.

LF

TOOTHED WHALE

Blowhole (one in toothed whales)

Eye

Melon or forehead

Beak or rostrum

Teeth

Ear

Lower jaw

Flipper

DORSAL FINS

falcate

triangular

rounded

just for company. But, in the enormity of the sea, individuals of a species might lose each other entirely had they no active ability to communicate beyond the scant limits of vision and no social order to keep them together. The dimensions of the sea forced whales along evolutionary paths that ensured group cohesiveness: to a greater or lesser extent, all species of whales communicate, and all form social groups for at least part of their life cycle.

The astonishing acoustical talents of whales have been mentioned, but it is important to emphasize that they developed in response to the physical demands of the water environment. Below about 150 meters (500 feet), darkness prevails in the sea, and above that depth vision is limited to just a few meters in almost all waters. Echolocation of objects at distances far beyond the limits of vision is possible because sound travels very efficiently in sea water, and does so at about five times the speed of sound in air. The acoustic situation is not simple, however. Sound waves bend or refract when they pass through the boundaries of layers of water caused by differences in temperature, pressure, or salinity. Temperature and pressure change with depth in the ocean, and salinity may vary from place to place as well as layer to layer, so refraction must be dealt with if echolocation is to function well. Also, if either the target (prey) or the echolocator is moving, shifts in the frequencies of the echos perceived will be caused by what is known as the Doppler effect. These shifts can yield precise information about the relative speed and orientation of objects in three dimensions, if they can be interpreted. Certainly the effective use of sound by whales suggests that they possess an exquisite working awareness of the physics of sound in water. Their loquaciousness in social contexts suggests, in addition, a communicative ability that in some ways may be better than ours, at least in potential "bits" of information communicated and the speed of their transmission. Probably the bulk of the cetacean brain is devoted to the rapid assimilation and mental solution of these

physics problems. Computer tests of cetacean abilities to discriminate signals and communicate are only now being attempted, and the results are eagerly awaited. In an almost longing way, we humans want to find higher meaning in cetacean sounds, but we must not let ourselves give them human meanings in human contexts.

Most whales see quite well in air, a carry-over from their ancestors' land-dwelling days. Whenever a whale wants to see objects on nearby land or in boats, it simply raises its head above the water and looks. This maneuver, called "spyhopping," may allow a whale to scrutinize objects of concern, investigate disturbances such as passing ships and other noisy machinery that invade its acoustic senses, or it may permit it to navigate by coastlines. Whales seem to spyhop for other reasons as well. Gray whales, for instance, may raise their head above the water to get a gravitational assist when swallowing a mouthful of bottom organisms or debris. Often they do not even raise the eyes above water, in which case it is certainly unlikely they are looking around.

Whales also may leap partly or completely out of the water—an activity called "breaching." Breaching may allow an animal an excellent airborne view (if it opens its eyes), it may serve to shake off small parasites clinging to the skin, or the loud splash may serve as some sort of signal to other whales. Or, maybe, it is simply fun and good exercise to jump and make a big splash. Humpback whale calves, for example, seem to breach as a form of play or in excitement.

Whales also splash the water with their fins and flukes, activities called, respectively, "finning" or "flippering" and "lobtailing." In these maneuvers the animal seems to try to strike its appendage flat against the water, producing a noise that can be heard in air for great distances on a calm day. Lobtailing and finning may play a role in feeding. Groups of dolphins and killer whales have been known to fin and lobtail when herding prey species. Sometimes part of a group will lobtail and splash while the others feed; the roles are then reversed, giving all members of the group an opportunity to feed. Evidently, prey species' freedom to move and escape capture in the sea has encouraged social coordination and organization among their cetacean predators.

Some cetacean social activity appears to be directed toward purposes other than feeding, for example, mating and the rearing of young. For both activities the details of social structure vary with the species. Whales of a number of species are known to take many mates during their lifetimes. Some may take only one, but none have been proven to be strictly monogamous in spite of popular stories to the contrary.

Many whale species have never been observed in courtship and mating activities. However, in mating, all cetaceans face the same general problems. Without arms to grasp and hold tight to one another in the rolling seas, cetacean copulation could be difficult and clumsy were it not for the fact that nature has provided the males with a penis that is essentially prehensile. It is strongly tapered toward the end and has the ability to roll and flex at the tip, permitting it to maneuver itself across the female's blubbery skin until it locates the vagina. It is also a very substantial structure, built to withstand the enormous torque created by the sweeping flukes and rolling bodies of the mating couple. In some species, such as the gray whale, sexual efforts may be assisted (or perhaps interfered with) by a second (or even a third or fourth) male who may push against the female and prevent her escape. This "assistance" may not be so much to help the other male as to increase one's own chances of coitus if the female has no escape and submits. Dolphins usually accomplish their copulation without such "assistance," and they may repeat coitus frequently for days, months, or even years. In fact, from observing them in captivity one might wonder if they ever do much else—and they might wonder if there will ever be much else to do. Even in the wild, there is frequent sexual activity between many members of a school, with no apparent taboos concerning the relationship (sometimes even the species) of the participants. Much of this sexual activity has no reproductive significance, as it occurs whether or not the females are in oestrus or breeding condition. This suggests that, as in primates, sexual activity may be important in the social bonding of herdmates and group members.

As with mating, details concerning the rearing of offspring are lacking for many species. The young of some species accompany their mothers for only six months to a year while they nurse; others receive parental care and guidance for many years after weaning. Many species of whales seem to exhibit great tenderness and concern for their young. Some species are legendary for the ferocity with which they defend their young, even in the face of such overwhelming danger as that presented by whalers.

It is, perhaps, this sense of parental care, of responsibility, almost, together with their apparent intelligence, curiosity, and inoffensiveness that has always drawn us to the whales. Awed by their size, dismayed by the prospect of ever understanding their way of life in a formidable habitat, we nonetheless are fascinated by these animals, with which we feel such an unlikely kinship. The great rise in popularity of whale watching in Hawaii, California, and New England bears eloquent witness to our desire to see and know the whales. For all that, we know lamentably little about them. Several species of great whales have been depleted to the point of near-extinction—for oil, fertilizer, pet food, cosmetics—before we have learned as much about them as we have about the rarest and most protected of land mammals. If we are to preserve the whales—and we have no excuse not to—then we must learn more about their astonishing abilities—and their weaknesses. It is to that greater knowledge and the hope for the whales' survival at our hands that the following pages are devoted.

A humpback whale blows, creating a rainbow.

BALEEN WHALES
SUBORDER: MYSTICETI

RORQUAL WHALES
FAMILY: BALAENOPTERIDAE

blue whale   fin whale   sei whale   Bryde's whale   minke whale   humpback whale

A S A GROUP the Balaenopteridae are the largest creatures ever to inhabit the earth. They are also the most modern—that is, the most recently evolved—of all whales.

Until the advent of modern whaling it appeared that the Balaenopteridae's evolutionary path was highly successful. Not only did these whales grow to prodigious size, but they flourished in great abundance throughout the world's temperate seas. Giant among giants, the blue whale (*Balaenoptera musculus*) formerly reached 30.5 m (100 ft) in length and had a worldwide population in excess of 400,000 animals. The fin whale (*Balaenoptera physalus*) reached more than 24.5 m (80 ft) with a worldwide population of more than 900,000 individuals. But over the past 80 years whalers have reduced the number of blues in the world to fewer than 25,000 and the number of fins to fewer than 150,000. Moreover, because whalers take large specimens by preference, the largest have been removed from the herds methodically; now, blue whales rarely grow larger than 24.5 m (80 ft) and fins as long as 18.5 m (60 ft) are exceedingly uncommon.

The modern history of the humpback whale (*Megaptera novaeangliae*) is even more depressing, although the few remaining herds have been afforded protection by most countries and seem to be holding their own.

Because they are smaller animals with less material to offer the whaler, the sei whale (*Balaenoptera borealis*), Bryde's whale (*Balaenoptera edeni*), and the minke whale (*Balaenoptera acutorostrata*) were not hunted as heavily as their larger cousins in the past. Recently however, as the larger whales have become increasingly scarce, the smaller Balaenopteridae also have been exploited to varying degrees by whalers.

The Balaenopteridae are distinguished from other baleen whales by pleated throat grooves that expand when the whales feed, permitting them to engorge great mouthfuls of food and water at a single gulp. In addition to this anatomical adaptation, evidence suggests that these animals can conceptualize their feeding approach—that they can perceive a desired result and organize a method for accomplishing it that goes far beyond grasping and swallowing a single prey, or straining a soup of plankton through baleen plates. The fin whale, for example, swims in rapid, clockwise circles around a school of food fish. When the school balls up, or compacts, to avoid the flashing white color on the right side of the whale's head, the fin lunges through the dense mass with its parachute-sized mouth agape, engulfing the prey it has corralled.

The humpback's feeding behavior is even more remarkable than that of the fin. Once the humpback locates a school of small fish or plankton, it swims in a slow spiral beneath the school, exhaling as it rises. In this way the whale builds a net, or screen, of bubbles around its prey. As the school tightens ranks in the center of the bubble net, the humpback swims up the bubble column with its mouth open, taking at a single gulp virtually the entire school.

We know little about the intricacies of these whales' social lives, but what we have been able to observe so far suggests that feeding is not the only realm in which the Balaenopteridae exhibit sophisticated behavior. It appears that specific groups of whales live together for most of their lives. Some researchers think they may mate for life, although this thesis cannot be proven on the basis of existing information. The maternal bond is known to be intense even in the face of mortal danger. And while mother Balaenopteridae surely guide their young through the rigors of juvenile life and teach them the necessary survival skills for life in the sea, whale calves just as surely have the ability to learn from their mothers, from other whales of their species, and from their own experiences.

Fin whales are very social animals, often traveling in groups of a dozen or more.

BLUE WHALE

sulphurbottom

Family **Balaenopteridae**
Genus *Balaenoptera*
Species ***B. musculus*** (Linnaeus, 1758)

It is scarcely possible to imagine the immense size of the blue whale. It is the largest known animal ever to inhabit the earth, exceeding even the great dinosaurs. Adult blue whales grow to more than 27.4 m (90 ft) long and may weigh more than 136,000 kg (150 tons). The blue whale's mouth can be 6 m (20 ft) long, its flippers 3 m (10 ft) long, and its flukes 4.5 m (15 ft) from tip to tip. Its heart is the size of a Volkswagen Beetle and pumps 9,700 kg (10.7 tons) of blood throughout the massive body in vessels so large that a human could crawl through the aorta. The blue whale's brain exceeds 7 kg (15 lb) and its stomach is large enough to hold over 1,800 kg (2 tons) of krill, the largest species of which, *Euphausia superba*, reaches only 5 cm (2 in) in length. A full-grown adult blue whale requires 1,800 kg (2 tons) of food per day to maintain its metabolic level. For all its size, the blue whale is an agile animal, and can maneuver well in close quarters.

Blue whales are an endangered species, having been hunted extensively over many decades. However, small herds exist in several regions of the world.

Physical description: Very broad body. The rostrum, like a broad, pointed arch when seen from above, has one large ridge extending from the tip to the blowholes and, occasionally, two very small and inconspicuous ridges, one on each side of the large central ridge. The region around and including the blowholes is raised above the dorsal region.

Color: The overall color is blue-gray, mottled with gray-white. Accumulated cold-water diatoms produce a yellow ventral region on some animals, giving the species its principal alternate name, "sulphurbottom."

Fins and flukes: Extremely small, ordinarily falcate dorsal fin is located three-quarters of the way down the body; it appears as the termination point of a lengthy dorsal ridge. Long thin flippers are well developed with a curvature along the leading margins, a feature unique among the rorqual whales. The flukes are relatively small, slightly rounded at their tips, with a median notch.

Length and weight: The largest blue captured reportedly measured 33.5 m (110 ft), although the average prewhaling, full-grown adult more likely measured 26 to 27.5 m (85 to 90 ft) long. Large blue whales have been so severely reduced in numbers by commercial whaling that the average size today is between 23 to 24.5 m (75 to 80 ft). (Females grow larger than males.) Although the largest blues at one time may have exceeded 136,000 kg (150 tons), today's average 100,000 kg (110 tons).

Throat grooves: More than 40 ventral grooves extend to the navel.

Baleen plates: More than 300 baleen plates line each side of the upper jaw. Usually they are all black, but photographs confirm occasional lighter coloration.

Feeding: Small euphausids in Southern Hemisphere; euphausids, other crustaceans, and small schooling fish in Northern Hemisphere.

Breathing and diving: Twelve to 14 shallow dives at 10- to 20-second intervals are followed by a longer and presumably deeper dive averaging 10 to 20 minutes, although it may last up to 50 minutes. Blues can dive to at least 110 m (350 ft). The blow produces a 9 m (30 ft) tall, slender, vertical spout similar to that of the humpback whale (page 56).

Mating and breeding: Calves, 7.5 m (25 ft), weighing 6,800 kg (7.5 tons), are born after an 11.25-month gestation period. A calf suckles about 380 liters (100 gallons) of milk, gaining more than 90kg (200 lb), per day. At weaning after 7 months, the calf is approximately 16 m (53 ft) long and weighs about 21,000 kg (23 tons). Sexual maturity is attained at about 5 to 7 years, when males average 22.5 m (74 ft) and females average 24 m (78 ft). Calving occurs at intervals of 2 to 3 years.

Herding: Blue whales are found individually or in groups of up to several dozen spread out over many miles. Pairs are very common.

Distribution: Small numbers of blue whales may be found in all oceans of the world.

Migration: Northern Hemisphere populations move north to polar regions in the spring; Southern Hemisphere populations move south to polar regions in autumn.

Natural history notes: While reports of blue whales breaching are rare, whale observers Stanley Minasian, Richard Sears, Lloyd Parker, and pilot Bill Riffe observed a series of spectacular breaches from the air 10 miles northeast of Danzante Island in Mexico's Sea of Cortez in March 1983. Two blue whales were observed, one estimated at 21 m (70 ft) and a smaller animal estimated at 17 m (56 ft). The smaller animal breached five to eight times, each time at a 45-degree angle, always landing on its stomach. The breaches reduced in intensity until finally only head slapping occurred, followed by normal breathing patterns. It has been suggested that blue whales live to at least 60 years of age.

A blue whale with throat pleats distended surfaces from a dive for food. Filtering a large mouthful of water through its baleen, the blue whale is left with krill which it swallows.

Richard Sears, MICS

Robert Pitman

Birgit Winning

Top, a blue whale prepares for a long and deep dive, lifting its 4.5 m (15 ft) wide flukes high into the air.

Above, the face of a blue whale on the surface. Note that the throat grooves or pleats run not only along the whale's underside but also along the mouth and under the eyes.

Right, often traveling alone or in pairs, blue whales are identified by their mottled blue color and light chevron-shaped pattern on the back behind the head.

Bernie Tershey & Craig Strong

Lloyd Parker

Above, the nostrils or blowholes of a blue whale. Note the extreme width of the head, unique among rorquals. When the whale breathes, muscles in the head expand the blowholes; underwater, they streamline to the contour of the head.

Right, the column-shaped blow of a blue whale may exceed 9 m (30 ft) in height.

FIN WHALE

Family **Balaenopertidae**
Genus *Balaenoptera*
Species ***B. physalus***   (Linnaeus, 1758)

With its long streamlined body, its gracefully pointed face, and its thin flukes, the fin whale might be considered to have classic rorqual features. Fin whales are the only cetaceans asymmetrically colored; the right side of a fin whale's lower jaw and its right baleen plates are white, while those of the left side are dark. They are fast and agile swimmers and work in pairs to round up and capture schools of fish. It is suspected that the light patch on the side of this whale's face may play a role in its feeding behavior. They are shy animals, compared to Bryde's and minke whales, which are known for their tendency to approach boats and ships. Fin whales have been observed swimming with blue whales in some areas, including the Gulf of St. Lawrence. Fin whales seldom lift their flukes prior to their lengthy dives, and they are not inclined to leap from the water as do others of their family.

Physical description: The body is long and slender. The rostrum closely resembles that of the blue whale but is thinner, more pointed, and always has a single central ridge. Fifty to 100 tactile hairs are found on the tips of the upper and lower jaws, with a distinctive clump of hairs at the tip of the lower jaw.

Color: Dark gray to brown dorsal and flank regions lighten to white ventral area. Dark dorsal coloration extends farther down on the left side than the right, a feature unique among cetaceans. Inside and outside of the right lower lip, and sometimes the upper lip as well, are yellow-white; the whalebone plates in that region are also yellow-white, while all other plates are yellow-gray. On most animals a gray-white chevron is located along the back and just behind the head.

Fins and flukes: Prominent falcate dorsal fin 60 cm (2 ft) high is located far back on the dorsal ridge. Flippers are thin and pointed at the tips. The flukes are nearly identical to those of the blue whale: large, thin, pointed at tips, very well defined, with a definite median notch.

Length and weight: Fin whales reach 27 m (88 ft) and 73,000 kg (80 tons). Average length is 20 m (64.5 ft). Females are slightly larger than males. Fin whales in the Northern Hemisphere average about 1.5 m (5 ft) smaller at maturity than those of the Southern Hemisphere.

Throat grooves: Fifty to 100 ventral grooves about 7.5 cm (3 in) apart extend slightly beyond the navel.

Baleen plates: There are 350 to 360 baleen plates on each side of the upper jaw averaging 90 cm (36 in) long, bluish-gray to white in color.

Feeding: Small crustaceans. North Atlantic populations also feed on capelin. North Pacific populations feed on small pelagic fish such as mackerel, tomcod, herring, saury, and even squid.

Breathing and diving: Five to 6 breaths at intervals of several minutes preceding dive lasting up to 15 minutes. A fin can dive at least 230 m (755 ft). The blow, 4.5 to 6 m (15 to 20 ft), resembles an inverted cone. These whales very seldom raise their flukes prior to long dives.

Mating and breeding: The calf, 6.5 m (21 ft) long, weighing 3,600 kg (4 tons), is born after an 11.5-month gestation. It is weaned after about 6 to 7 months when it has reached 12 m (39 ft). Sexual maturity is attained at 10 to 13 years when males are about 18.5 m (60 ft), females about 19.8 m (65 ft) long. Calving occurs at 2 to 3 year intervals. They are thought to be monogamous; much affectionate behavior is exhibited.

Herding: Often observed in groups exceeding 100, but normally singly to 10 animals.

Distribution: Fins inhabit all oceans, although they apparently avoid shallow waters and coastal regions. They frequent approximately the same waters as blue whales. The largest population seems to be in Antarctic waters.

Migration: Apparently these whales feed in cold-water regions during summer and return to warm waters for mating and breeding in winter. It has been noted that migration is irregular, perhaps because fins are following food fish.

Natural history notes: Fin whales are thought to live to between 75 and 100 years.

An adult fin whale swims into a dye marker placed in the water for fisheries research. The white color on the right side of the jaw is clearly visible.

Richard Sears, MICS

Kenneth C. Balcomb, III

Left, a fin whale swims rapidly on its right side with mouth open, "lunge-feeding" in the Gulf of California.

Top, fin whales are cosmopolitan, sometimes seen near centers of human population as well as more remote places. This group was photographed in Canada's St. Lawrence River estuary.

Above, ready to blow, a fin whale rises to the surface off the coast of Nova Scotia. Note the complex color patterns on the fin's head.

SEI WHALE

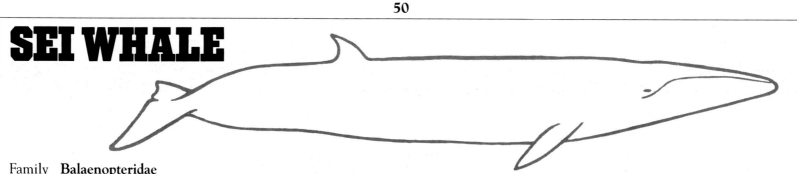

Family **Balaenopteridae**
Genus *Balaenoptera*
Species ***B. borealis***   Lesson, 1828

Taxonomic note: Southern Hemisphere animals, which may be somewhat larger than Northern Hemisphere animals, are incorrectly classified as *Balaenoptera schlegeli*.

Probably the fastest of all whales, the sei can reach speeds in excess of 38 kph (24 mph) which may assist them in capturing the small schooling fish on which they prefer to feed. Sei whales feed on euphausids and other crustaceans which they catch while swimming on the surface, mouth open, skimming the water much as right whales do. Sei whales rise horizontally to the surface to breathe, exposing the dorsal fin and head simultaneously.

This whale derived its name from "seje," a Norwegian term for pollack, a member of the codfish family, because the whales appeared off Norway simultaneously with schools of the fish.

Physical description: One long ridge runs from the tip of the upper jaw to the blowholes. The tip of the rostrum is more rounded than that of the fin whale.

Color: Smooth dark gray on dorsal and flank regions, and the posterior ventral region as well. Numerous white oval marks on flanks and ventral surface are scars caused by lamprey and cookie-cutter shark bites. The body seems to have a galvanized appearance. The chin, throat, and belly are white as far back as at least the end of the throat grooves. Small white dots may be present on dark lower ventral region. Flippers and flukes are dark gray.

Fins and flukes: The falcate dorsal fin is very tall (25 to 61 cm or 10 to 24 in) and situated farther back than that of the fin whale. The flippers are large, thin, rounded at the trailing edge, and pointed at the tips. The flukes are disproportionately small, and pointed at the tips. There is a definite median notch.

Length and weight: Males may exceed 18 m (60 ft) in length and weigh 22,000 kg (24 tons); females may exceed 20 m (65 ft) and 24,000 kg (26 tons).

Throat grooves: Sei whales possess 38 to 56 throat grooves spaced about 7.5 cm (3 in) apart, extending down the throat to between the flippers.

Baleen plates: There are 320 to 380 baleen plates on each side of the upper jaw with fine white bristles. The plates measure up to 78.7 cm (31 in) in length.

Feeding: Sei whales prefer euphausids and other small crustaceans, but also feed on capelin, pollack, anchovies, herring, cod, and sardines. No bottom-dwelling organisms are taken.

Breathing and diving: They blow 2 to 3 times at approximately 17-second intervals before a 5- to 10-minute dive. They rise to the surface horizontally and do not expose their flukes prior to their long dive. The blow resembles an inverted cone, rarely taller than 4.5 m (15 ft).

Mating and breeding: A 4.5 to 5 m (15 to 16 ft), 900 kg (1 ton) calf is born after an 11-month gestation period. Sexual maturity is reached at 8 years when males are 13 m (43 ft) and females are 13.7 m (45 ft) long. Calving takes place at 2-year intervals.

Herding: Usually observed alone or in pairs; groups of up to 50 have been observed where food is plentiful.

Distribution: They are found in all oceans but seem to avoid ice packs.

Migration: They are known to follow the movements of food fish, making migration routes unpredictable.

Natural history notes: It is thought that sei whales live to at least 70 years of age.

Right, a head-on photograph of a sei whale reveals the wide placement of the eyes and very sharp rostrum—the combination probably gives the whale binocular vision.

Below, a sei whale breaks the surface, cruising the tropical Pacific. While the sei whale and Bryde's whale look similar from a distance, seis have a much taller dorsal fin and only one ridge on their rostrum while Bryde's have three.

Kenneth C. Balcomb, III

BRYDE'S WHALE

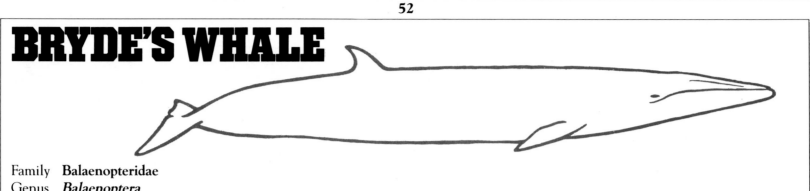

Family **Balaenopteridae**
Genus *Balaenoptera*
Species ***B. edeni*** Anderson, 1878

Bryde's whales inhabit the tropical and subtropical oceans of the world and are naturally not as numerous as the other rorqual species because food is less abundant in tropical waters. They are often confused with sei whales, but can be distinguished by the three prominent ridges usually present on their heads. If close-up inspection is possible, the coarse gray baleen and ventral throat pleats extending to or beyond the navel are additional characteristics that identify Bryde's whales. These whales are rather solitary in their habits, usually keeping their distance from each other even when there is a local abundance of food.

Oceanographers from the Galapagos Islands report a Bryde's whale encounter in 1979, during which the whale approached a small sailboat closely enough to be touched and stroked.

Bryde's whales were named after Captain Johan Bryde, who established South Africa's first whaling station.

Physical description: The Bryde's whale can be identified positively at close quarters by two secondary ridges on top of the rostrum, one on either side of the central ridge.

Color: Dark gray dorsally, lighter color ventrally. Occasionally dotted with small, oval white scars presumably caused by cookie-cutter shark bites. Some individuals possess a much lighter region on both sides forward of dorsal fin. Right lower lip region is dark gray. Dark band runs across stomach.

Fins and flukes: Small dorsal fin (45 cm or 18 in) is very falcate and situated at the extreme rear of the midback region, although farther forward than that of some other whales. It often appears tattered or notched along the hind margin. Flippers are medium-sized and thin, very well developed and somewhat rounded at tips. Flukes are almost identical to those of the blue whale (page 40): large, thin, pointed at tips, and very well defined, with a definite median notch.

Length and weight: Bryde's whales reach 14.6 m (48 ft) and 20,000 kg (22 tons).

Throat grooves: About 45 ventral throat grooves extend to navel.

Baleen plates: Approximately 300 plates on each side of upper jaw, slate gray with coarse dark-colored bristles up to 46 cm (18 in) long.

Feeding: Schooling fish such as pilchard, sardine, and saury, as well as crustaceans and squid.

Breathing and diving: Several moderately high blows of about 3.5 m (11 ft) after a dive of 8 to 15 minutes. These are very fast and agile whales. Their pursuit of prey does not generally require deep dives, and they can be spotted by slicks of turbulence (tracks) at the surface that indicate they are swimming at 15 to 30 m (50 to 100 ft) deep. The dorsal fin usually appears after the blowholes have submerged due to the steep angle of rising and diving in this relatively deep-diving species.

Mating and breeding: The calf, 4.3 m (14 ft), 900 kg (1 ton), is born after 11.5-month gestation. Males attain sexual maturity at 8 to 13 years when about 12 m (39 ft); females at 7 to 10 years when about 13 m (43 ft).

Herding: Individually or in groups of up to 10. One large herd up to 100 has been confirmed. Normally well dispersed.

Distribution: Found in the tropical and subtropical waters of the North Pacific, Central Pacific, South Atlantic, and Indian oceans between 40° north and 40° south latitudes.

Migration: Commonly believed not to migrate.

Natural history notes: Bryde's whales are believed to live to about 40 years. They are known to breach.

Michael Graybill

Above, this Bryde's whale displays its characteristic three-ridge rostrum—a central ridge flanked by two smaller ridges.

Right, feeding on the surface, an adult Bryde's whale exposes an eye. Its throat grooves are visible below the lower jaw.

MINKE WHALE

little piked whale lesser rorqual

Family **Balaenopteridae**
Genus *Balaenoptera*
Species ***B. acutorostrata***   Lacépède, 1804

Taxonomic note: Minke whales inhabiting the waters around Sri Lanka are occasionally classified as *Balaenoptera acutorostrata thalmaha*. Those inhabiting the Southern Hemisphere, with a gray instead of a white patch on the flippers, are occasionally classified as *Balaenoptera bonaerensis*.

The smallest of the rorqual whales, the minke is not much larger than the largest member of the dolphin family, the killer whale. Unlike most other rorquals, minke whales will approach and swim around boats and ships at sea. Minke whales are often observed leaping clear of the water, exposing their entire bodies, and on at least one occasion a minke was seen riding the bow-wave of a ship in much the same way a dolphin would. Nonetheless, it is a difficult whale to observe at sea, for its blow is quick and inconspicuous.

Physical description: The rostrum is pointed with lower jaw protruding. The forehead has a single, prominent, convex ridge from the tip of the rostrum to the blowhole.

Color: The dorsal region is black from the tip of the rostrum (occasionally including lower lips) to just behind the flippers, merging to a slightly lighter shade which gradually becomes black again at the flukes. The ventral region is white from throat to anus. Flippers are black with a distinctive white band which varies in intensity with individuals and geographic location. The dorsal fin is black. Most Pacific animals have a light gray chevron extending from flank to flank just above the flippers.

Fins and flukes: A well-developed, falcate dorsal fin is situated about two-thirds back on the body. Flippers are long, thin, and pointed at tips. Flukes are relatively large, thin, and pointed at tips, with a definite median notch.

Length and weight: Minkes grow to about 9 m (30 ft) and 9,000 kg (10 tons). Southern Hemisphere animals are slightly larger than their Northern Hemisphere counterparts.

Throat grooves: Fifty to 70 ventral grooves are present, extending from the chin to near the navel.

Baleen plates: Minkes possess between 280 and 300 creamy white plates on each side of the upper jaw, sometimes fringed with dark brown. They reach a length of about 28 cm (11 in).

Feeding: Small shoaling fish (herring, cod, capelin, pollack), krill, and copepods.

Breathing and diving: They take 5 to 10 breaths between shallow dives, preceding a longer, presumably deeper dive lasting up to 10 minutes. Before the longer dive, the animal arches its back but does not expose its flukes. The blow is quick and inconspicuous.

Mating and breeding: A 3 m (10 ft), 450 kg (1,000 lb) calf is born after a gestation period of between 10 and 11 months. Mothers lactate less than 6 months. Sexual maturity is attained at about 6 years when the males are 7 m (23 ft) and the females 7.3 m (24 ft). Females are thought to bear young at least every other year.

Herding: Usually found alone but often observed in small groups of up to 6 animals.

Distribution: Minkes are found in all oceans, with concentrations in temperate waters. Rarely observed in the tropics.

Migration: Minkes are inshore animals, although they occasionally venture into the open ocean. Herds occur in higher latitudes during summer; they return to warmer waters during the winter.

Natural history notes: Minkes are believed to live as long as 50 years. At times they can be extremely inquisitive, approaching small boats closely enough to be touched.

Gordon Williamson

Above, a non-parasitical fish with a suction disk on its head, the remora frequently attaches itself to large fish and whales. Here a number of remoras hitch a ride on a minke whale.

Opposite, a minke whale breaches, leaping almost completely out of the water and showing its characteristically pure white flipper band. Among the most active and inquisitive of all great whales, breaching minkes rise out of the water at an angle, dorsal-side up, and re-enter without spinning or turning their bodies.

HUMPBACK WHALE

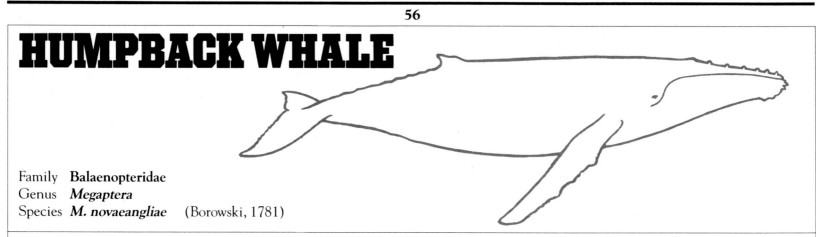

Family **Balaenopteridae**
Genus *Megaptera*
Species *M. novaeangliae*   (Borowski, 1781)

The only external similarity between the humpback whale and other rorquals is the throat grooves, which extend from the chin to the navel. This whale is not long and sleek; its body is rounded, narrowing to a slender peduncle whose flukes, sharply serrated on the trailing edge, are unique among whales. The humpback's facial characteristics are also unique because of the many knobs or protuberances containing hair follicles. Its flippers are one-third the length of the body, the longest among all cetaceans, and are knobby along the leading edge where finger bones end. The leading edges of the flippers often are covered with sharp barnacles. The flippers are highly flexible and mobile, and capable of dramatic gyrations when the animals breach.

The humpback is best known for its vocalizations, which cover many octaves and include frequencies beyond the threshold of human hearing. Humpback songs, apparently sung only by lone males, last as long as 20 minutes, after which they are repeated, often with slight changes. The songs occur only in those warm-water regions to which the animals migrate for breeding, and change from season to season, varying subtly among groups.

Recent experiences by divers in Hawaiian waters have shown humpbacks to be both aware and cautious of the human visitors but without the slightest trace of hostility. The whales were careful to avoid collisions or other mishaps when divers approached.

Physical description: The upper and lower edges of the mouth and the dorsal ridge from the blowhole to the tip of the jaw are covered with hair follicles set in conspicuous, rounded bumps. Charles Jurasz, noted humpback whale researcher, theorizes that only males possess knucklelike bumps running along the dorsal ridge behind the dorsal fin.

Color: Humpbacks are black all over except for parts of the underside including the chin, throat, chest, belly, and the flukes. The flippers vary from all black to all white. The white on the underside of the flukes assists researchers in positive identification of individual animals, as the patterns exposed when the tail is lifted for a dive are unique to each whale. Often the entire body may be covered with small scratches, presumably from physical contact with other barnacle-encrusted humpbacks.

Fins and flukes: The dorsal fin is situated more than two-thirds of the way down the back, and varies in size and shape from one animal to another; it is usually small and may be barely discernible or large and falcate. The flippers are about one-third

the body length, extremely mobile and used for underwater maneuvering, among other things. The wide flukes are serrated and pointed at the tips. There is a definite median notch.

Length and weight: Humpbacks reach 19 m (62 ft) in length and weigh in excess of 48,000 kg (53 tons). Northern Hemisphere animals are slightly shorter than their Southern Hemisphere counterparts.

Throat grooves: There are between 14 and 24 ventral grooves present, 13 to 20 cm (5 to 8 in) apart and extending slightly beyond the navel.

Baleen plates: There are 350 to 370 baleen plates on each side of the upper jaw; blackish-brown in color. They reach 60 cm (24 in) in length.

Feeding: Apparently feed only while in cold water. Their diet includes krill, plankton, sardine, saury, mackerel, anchovy, capelin, and other schooling small fish. Humpbacks in Glacier Bay, Alaska,

have been documented blowing underwater bubble circles to entrap plankton. They then swim up through the swarm, mouth agape, taking in large quantities of food.

Breathing and diving: They remain on the surface for from 3 to 6 minutes between long dives, breathing at 15- to 30-second intervals. A longer dive follows, marked often by the raising of the tail high into the air. Although this longer dive may last as long as 30 minutes, it is not necessarily a deep dive as underwater observation confirms that humpbacks dive vertically from the surface and often remain within several body lengths of it, twisting and rolling, often in close physical contact with one or more other animals. The humpback's blow is tall, thin, and very obvious.

Mating and breeding: Calves are born 4 to 4.3 m (13 to 14 ft) in length after a gestation period believed to be 11.5 months. Mating and birthing takes place every second or third year, and calves may exceed 8 m (26 ft) when weaned seven months after birth. Sexual maturity is attained in males when they are 11.5 m (38 ft) long; females

J. Michael Williamson

when they are 12 m (39 ft) long. Physical maturity is attained at 14 to 30 years when males are 13 m (43 ft) long and females 13.7 m (45 ft).

Herding: They herd in groups of about a dozen on calving grounds, or in smaller groups of 3 to 4 separated by many miles during migration. It is not uncommon however, to observe individuals and pairs on calving grounds. The newborn often stays in close proximity to the mother. When swimming, newborns have been observed to ride the mother's slipstream as she swims. Adult and calf seem to be separated often from the main herd, accompanied by a second adult believed to be the father.

Distribution: They are found in all oceans to the edge of the ice but follow definite migratory routes. They occur in the polar regions for half of the year and warmer waters during the remaining time.

There appear to be three geographically isolated populations—North Pacific, North Atlantic, and Southern Hemisphere—each composed of several discrete stocks.

Migration: Some Southern Hemisphere stocks migrate during the winter from Antarctic waters to South African waters; some move up the coast of South America. Others travel north into the waters of New Zealand, Australia, the Fiji Islands, New Caledonia, and the New Hebrides. It is thought that some humpback populations from Greenland and the Barents Sea migrate south along the European coast into the upper North Atlantic waters, while others from the south of Greenland migrate through the western North Atlantic to Bermuda and the West Indies. Populations from the Bering and Chukchi seas migrate south along the North American coastline then west to Hawaii.

Natural history notes: Humpbacks normally travel at between 4 and 9.5 kph (2.5 and 6 mph), but they can maintain speeds in excess of 19 kph (12 mph) for short periods of time. Belying their reputation as "gentle giants," humpback males engage in severe fights in mating areas that often result in extensive scratching, scarring, and, on at least one occasion, bleeding. These fights determine which males will mate with and/or accompany females.

This spectacular photograph is of a humpback whale breaching off the coast of New England.

58

Champion breachers, humpbacks such as this one leap and spin in the air, often returning with a mighty splash audible miles away.

A diver takes the measurements of a humpback whale caught in a fish net. Trapped in Trinity Bay, Newfoundland, this animal was successfully released.

Opposite, small populations of humpbacks such as this pair, migrate to Hawaii each February; they present the only opportunity for the comeback of this once severely hunted and still endangered species.

Kenneth C. Balcomb, III

Kenneth C. Balcomb, III

Deborah Glockner-Ferrari

Steve Peake/Photo Researchers, Inc.

Humpback whales engage in a spectacular feeding strategy called "bubble netting." After blowing a bubble net under a school of food fish, the whales rise open-mouthed through the concentrated school.

GRAY WHALE
FAMILY: ESCHRICHTIIDAE

ALTHOUGH the gray whale once roamed the coasts of both the North Atlantic and North Pacific oceans, its present range is restricted to the North Pacific and adjacent Arctic seas. Gray whales are inshore animals, generally inhabiting water less than 250 m (820 ft) deep. They are also migratory, presumably navigating by following learned routes over the bottom topography and perhaps by following coastal promontories.

The gray whale's long passage from summer feeding grounds in the Bering and Chukchi seas to calving and wintering grounds along the peninsula of Baja California in Mexico is the longest known annual migration for any mammal and is remarkably precise in its annual timing. Each autumn, as chill winds begin to whip across the Bering and Chukchi seas, and the ice pack moves down from the polar cap, thousands of grays abandon the shallow, food-rich Arctic waters and begin their journey toward the warm, protected lagoons of Baja California. There the pregnant females bear their young while other whales relax and swim around the lagoon entrances. In their migration, virtually all of these whales travel through Unimak Pass in the Aleutian chain, and most then follow the continental shelf south past southeast Alaska and British Columbia to Washington, where they encounter and follow the shoreline to Mexico, providing a spectacular sight for coastal residents and tourists who whale-watch from the headlands and coastal sight-seeing vessels.

Pregnant females lead the migration, then adult males and subadults of both sexes following the route that has become a ritual of the species. Gray whale counts at several strategic points along the migratory path indicate that about 16,000 individuals make up the eastern North Pacific stock—a substantial increase from the few thousand whales that survived the first three decades of the twentieth century, when modern whaling ravaged the population for a second time. (Gray whales had been nearly extirpated by American whalers earlier in the 1850s and 1860s.) The western North Pacific (or Korean) stock did not survive the recent era of intensive whaling in significant numbers and is now extinct or nearly so.

On the one hand the recovery of the eastern North Pacific gray whale is a notable achievement in conservation and a measure of the species' tenacious hold on existence. On the other hand, only a single stock of gray whales has survived the past few hundred years of human arrogance and rapacity, and there is no reason to believe there will be any others in the future of this planet. Contemporary threats to the remaining gray whales derive, not from the direct exploitation that destroyed their predecessors, but from contamination and usurpation of their highly restricted habitat, conditions that we still fail to acknowledge as our responsibility to control.

Breathing and diving in unison, gray whales often travel in groups of a dozen or more during their extended migrations.

GRAY WHALE

Family **Eschrichtiidae**
Genus *Eschrichtius*
Species *E. robustus*   (Lilljeborg, 1861)

The gray whale is unusual not only in that it has been assigned its own taxonomic family, but also in that, unlike most other large whales, it prefers shallow water to deep.

Because grays usually mate and calve in the lagoons of Baja California, they frequently come into close contact with humans. A century ago, this proximity, which made hunting the whales relatively easy, brought the gray to the edge of extinction. But over the past 40 years the eastern North Pacific population has virtually reestablished itself, and the whales' annual migration has become an ideal opportunity for their observation by cetologists and whale watchers. The recovery of the gray whale is particularly remarkable, as no other large whale has yet recovered to such an extent.

Gray whales feed on bottom organisms, filtering them through the coarsest sieving fibers of any baleen whale. Although gray whales have been observed "feeding" on kelp close to shore along the California coastline, closer observations suggest that they are in fact taking kelp fronds into their cavernous mouths with large quantities of water to sluice microorganisms from the fronds.

Physical description: The mouth is slightly bowed. The eyes are located just before and above the juncture of the jaws. There are more tactile hairs on the tips of the upper and lower jaws and on the forehead than on any other species of whale.

Color: Mottled gray overall, but infested on the dorsal region with the parasitic, crablike crustaceans called whale lice and barnacles, which may create numerous large yellow and white patches. The tongue is pink with a gray tip.

Fins and flukes: Instead of a dorsal fin there are 9 to 13 small knucklelike bumps along the dorsal ridge extending from past the midback region to the flukes. The flippers are well developed, paddle shaped, and pointed at the tips. The flukes are well spread, pointed at the tips, and have a definite median notch. Pieces of the flukes may be missing from individual grays; such injuries are thought to result from killer whale attacks.

Length and weight: Grays reach 13.7 to 15.2 m (45 to 50 ft) in length and may exceed 27,000 kg (30 tons). Females (especially their heads) are believed to be slightly larger than males.

Throat grooves: There are 2 to 4 large, thick furrows 1.5 m (5 ft) in length, extending the length of the throat. They apparently do not expand during feeding but instead may serve to enhance a pistonlike action of the tongue while the animal sucks up organisms from the ocean floor.

Baleen plates: There are 140 to 180 thick, yellow-white plates on each side of the upper jaw, up to 40 cm (16 in) in length, with very long, thick bristles.

Feeding: Grays feed on crustaceans, bottom-dwelling amphipods, small schooling fish, and microorganisms obtained from kelp fronds during migration. Kenneth S. Norris observed at least one gray whale submerging and surfacing in the surge outside a Baja California lagoon in what he felt might be a feeding behavior pattern, the whale allowing water to rush into its mouth for filtering.

Breathing and diving: Grays normally blow, or breathe, 3 to 5 times in rapid succession before a lengthy, presumably deep dive, usually between 5 and 7 minutes, although it may last as long as 18 minutes. The flukes often are raised into the air prior to a lengthier dive. The blow is forceful and obvious at long range; it appears bushy and U-shaped.

Mating and breeding: Mating occurs during the southern migration. Calves, 5 m (16 ft), weighing 500 kg (1,100 lb), are born after a 13-month gestation period, and weaned at 7 months when they reach about 8 m (27 ft) and 6,800 kg (7.5 tons). Sexual maturity is reached at between 5 and 11 years when males are 11 m (36 ft) and females 11.5 m (38 ft). Calving occurs every 2 years.

Herding: During the migration about 6 females with calves are thought to form a herd. Lone whales are observed during the beginning and middle of the migration south and are thought to be pregnant females. Other migrating groups of from 3 to 5 are made up of nonpregnant females usually accompanied by one or more males. The last to appear seem to be the previous year's newborn making the journey for the first time.

Distribution: Although the gray once was found in both the North Atlantic and North Pacific, now only the population of the eastern North Pacific survives.

Migration: From November through February the main population migrates south along the North American coastline to warm-water lagoons of Baja California—one of the longest migratory routes known for a mammal, covering 9,600 to 11,000 km (6,000 to 7,000 mi). The return trip to the Bering Sea begins during February and animals continue to be sighted from the northwest coast through June and July.

Marc Webber

Natural history notes: It is thought that gray whales live at least 50 years. In the mid-1970s several gray whales in San Ignacio Lagoon, Baja California, approached small boats and allowed themselves to be touched and petted. The number of gray whale "friendlies" has increased each year; this unusual and inexplicable behavior is now exhibited in Scammon's Lagoon, Baja California, and on at least one occasion has occurred in Puget Sound, Washington. (Personal communication, James Hudnall.)

So inquisitive they are nicknamed "friendlies," some gray whales such as this one in Baja California's San Ignacio Lagoon allow people to touch them.

Ronn Storro-Patterson

Opposite, the only known photograph of a baleen whale birth. Protruding from its mother's birth canal, a baby gray whale is born head first, and moments later swims free near its mother in Bocca Solidad, Baja California.

Above, a gray whale and its calf will stay close together for the first few months of the young whale's life. Note the brown trail of mud stirred up from the bottom of Scammon's Lagoon, Baja California.

Gerard Wellington

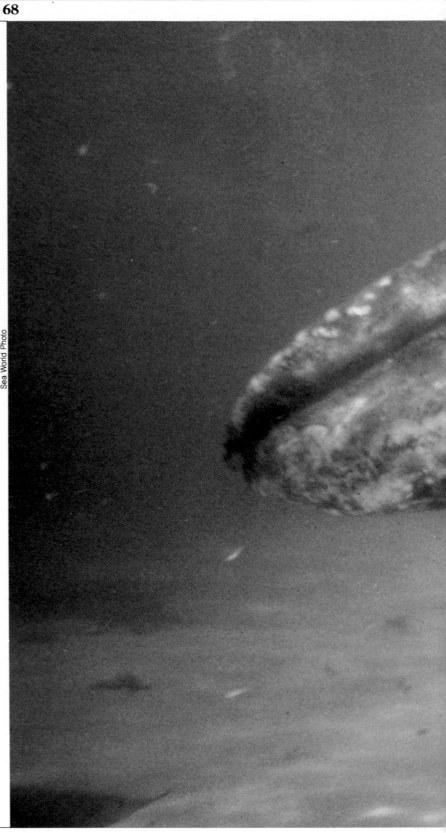

Sea World Photo

Above, a juvenile gray whale sluices a section of kelp fronds in its mouth, washes off the micro-organisms and swallows them. The kelp is released undamaged.

Right, Gigi, a gray whale captured in a Baja California lagoon in 1970, was the only great whale kept in captivity for any length of time. After a year, she was released into the wild.

RIGHT WHALES
FAMILY: BALAENIDAE

right whale
bowhead whale
pygmy right whale

RIGHT WHALES were once numerous, but because they are big, slow, extremely fat, and they float when they are killed, their numbers were severely reduced during the heyday of hand-harpoon whaling. Their worldwide populations have not yet recovered, and they remain extremely rare thoughout most of their former range. Modern whalers never have found enough of them to warrant serious pursuit, but they have been caught from time to time in this century.

Next to grubbing about on the sea floor for food like the gray whale, the simplest way for a baleen whale to make its living is to open its mouth and swim through dense concentrations of plankton. This is the manner in which the right whales feed. Accordingly, their mouths, which remain open almost continuously as they skim through patches of planktonic soup, have become enormous in the course of evolution, with tremendous surface areas of filtering baleen. Right whales can filter about 15 cubic meters (20 cubic yards) of water per minute, straining out the minute plankton prey species by the bushel and washing them down their gullets. A right whale's feeding sounds include what might be called a loud smacking of the lips as the baleen plates are shaken to dislodge the plankton from the hairlike fringe of the plates before swallowing. This sound, which can be heard for considerable distances in air and underwater, was dubbed "baleen rattle" by the scientists who first noted it.

There are three basic types of right whales extant. The bowhead, or Greenland right whale, evolved its lifestyle to live in the icy polar waters of the Northern Hemisphere, where plankton soup flourishes in summer months as the ice retreats. Although its population was decimated by Yankee whalers during the nineteenth century, the bowhead still survives and is currently taken in small numbers in a subsistence harvest by Arctic Eskimos.

The right whale is thought by some researchers to comprise two distinct species virtually indistinguishable from each other in appearance. One is indigenous to the Northern Hemisphere and the other to southern oceans. The right whales of each hemisphere migrate to high latitudes to feed, then return to temperate or tropical seas to breed and calve. A single population of at least 1,000 individuals wintering along the Argentine coast seems to be thriving, but even that group is just a remnant of a formerly abundant South Atlantic stock. Another population of perhaps fewer than 200 individuals winters along the coast of Georgia in the United States and summers in the waters off New England. It has not grown perceptibly in total numbers, but researchers have noted a few new calves in recent years. Some researchers believe that a factor in the right whales' slow recovery from whaling is that sei whales (see Balaenopteridae), which also possess fine baleen fringes and have a propensity for skimming plankton, may be competing for their feeding niche.

The third right whale is a pygmy version. Small, shy, and restricted to the Southern Hemisphere, it has never been hunted extensively, and its apparent lack of abundance seems to be due to its extreme evolutionary specialization rather than to overexploitation. There doesn't seem to be an ecological place for a diminutive cetacean skim-feeder of copepods. Some authors place the pygmy right whale in its own family: Neobalaenidae (Gray, 1847), but a monotypic family so closely related to the other right whales serves no useful taxonomic purpose, and it is generally not used.

Rotund and stocky, right whales, mother and calf pictured here, are slow swimmers and unafraid of divers.

RIGHT WHALE

black right whale

Family **Balaenidae**
Genus *Eubalaena*
Species *E. glacialis*   (Müller, 1776)

Taxonomic note: Geographically distinct populations are occasionally given their own subspecies classification, as follows: southern right whale, *Eubalaena glacialis australis*; North Pacific right whale, *Eubalaena glacialis japonica*; North Atlantic right whale, *Eubalaena glacialis glacialis*.

This stocky animal has large flippers and enormous, arching lower lips that cover and protect its long, delicate baleen plates. Right whales possess unique natural patches on the tip of the upper jaw, near the eyes and along the cheeks, called callosities. These growths are home for whale lice and, less frequently, barnacles, and vary in size and location with each individual allowing positive identification for researchers. Males possess larger and more numerous callosities than females.

Right whales are very slow swimmers and unafraid of divers who approach close enough for physical contact. Today, they are perhaps the rarest of the great whales and study of certain populations such as those which migrate to Patagonia each year indicates that the population is not increasing in numbers.

Courtship and mating among right whales may last for days, weeks, or even months at a time. Females can avoid mating, if they choose: they may swim upside down, raise the rear portion of their bodies out of the water, or out-maneuver rejected males.

One of the right whale's most fascinating habits is to raise its flukes into the air and use them as a sail, letting the wind move the animal through the water. Roger Payne, the first to report this activity, says that the animals will often swim back up to the beginning point in order to repeat the maneuver. Payne also describes the personalities of right whales as playful and mischievous, for any object placed in the water is quickly poked, pushed, and bumped. Such "toys" may include, as Dr. Payne notes, tide markers, inflatable boats, and even a specially built underwater observation vehicle.

Physical description: Right whales are extremely fat. The large bowed mouth and other parts of the head possess callosities—cornified growths inhabited by whale lice of a species which exists only on right whales. Often the skin of the back is observed peeling and sloughing off, making the animal appear unhealthy, although the condition is normal for all cetaceans.

Color: Black with white patches on the ventral region, particularly around the anus. Regions of the body may be mottled with brown.

Fins and flukes: Right whales have no dorsal fin. Their flippers are paddle shaped. The flukes are extremely wide, thin, pointed or slightly rounded at the tips, with a definite median notch.

Length and weight: Right whales occasionally reach 17.7 m (58 ft) and may exceed 90,000 kg (100 tons), although normally they are 15 m (50 ft) long and weigh about 64,000 kg (70 tons).

Baleen Plates: From 225 to 250 pairs of black baleen plates on each side of the upper jaw, with a maximum length of 2.2 m (7.2 ft).

Feeding: This species is a selective feeder taking mostly copepods and euphausids.

Breathing and diving: Right whales are very slow swimmers. They blow several times prior to a longer, presumably deeper dive lasting 10 to 20 minutes. Two separate spouts are visible, one from each nostril. They are capable of deep dives but are generally believed to remain in shallow waters.

Mating and breeding: Calves are born 5 to 6 m (16 to 19 ft) long in the winter after a gestation period believed to be 12 months. Newborns remain with their mothers for a full year with weaning when the calf has grown to about 8.5 m (28 ft). Sexual maturity in males is reached at 15 m (49 ft); at 16 m (52 ft) in females. Females are thought to give birth every third year.

Herding: Individuals to groups of up to five.

Distribution: The various alleged subspecies are found in all temperate oceans. The southern right whale is found throughout the Antarctic, southern waters of South America, southern waters of South Africa, Australia, New Zealand, South Georgia,

Jen & Des Bartlett, Courtesy Survival Anglia Ltd.

and also observed in the Indian Ocean and near the northern coast of Chile. The North Pacific right whale is found from Japan throughout the waters of Kamchatka Peninsula and the Aleutian Islands south throughout the waters of the states of Washington and Oregon as far down as Baja California. The North Atlantic right whale is found from Spitzbergen, Bear Island, and Nordkap as far south as Spain, Portugal, North Africa, the Carolinas, Florida, and the southern range of the Gulf of Mexico.

Migration: In the winter, the North Pacific and North Atlantic animals migrate to the southern ends of their range, and the southern animals migrate to the northern end of their range.

Mother and baby right whales maintain a close relationship clearly evident in this photograph taken off Patagonia, Argentina.

Chuck Nicklin

Jen & Des Bartlett, Courtesy Survival Anglia Ltd.

Above, two right whales mate in this rare photograph. Note the penis of the male on the left. Both animals are almost belly-up, allowing for easier intromission.

Left, a right whale moves along the surface with mouth open, skimming plankton and straining it through fine white baleen plates.

Opposite, right whale researchers can often identify individual right whales by their callosities, hardened patches of skin which vary from whale to whale.

BOWHEAD WHALE

Greenland right whale

Family **Balaenidae**
Genus ***Balaena***
Species ***B. mysticetus*** Linnaeus, 1758

Bowhead whales inhabit only arctic waters, where they follow the seasonal advance and retreat of the ice edge. Their populations have been severely reduced by whaling, making them the most endangered of all large whales. Their commercial value lay not only in a large yield of oil (70 to 90 barrels), but in baleen as well, for the manufacture of corsets and household brushes before the development of plastics. Bowheads were protected from commercial whaling in 1946, but the International Whaling Commission permitted an unregulated subsistence kill by or on behalf of Eskimos until recent years. The IWC now regulates the Eskimo kill. The U.S Marine Mammal Protection Act of 1972 also permitted subsistence hunting of these whales by Eskimos.

Their limited numbers and the harsh aquatic environment in which they live make them the most difficult of all large whales to study.

Like other members of its family, the bowhead is a stocky animal whose head comprises nearly one-third of its total body length. Its baleen plates are the longest of all whales. The white patch occurring on the bottom lip of many animals is irregularly shaped and found only on this species. With no dorsal fin on its thick, broad back, the bowhead is capable of breaking through new ice up to 30.5 cm (12 in) thick. This may be why these whales are often accompanied by belugas, for the small white whales must seek out breaks in the ice to breathe. Young bowheads remain submerged longer than older animals. Whether this activity is a function of age, hierarchical feeding position in the group, or something else remains open to conjecture. Bowhead whales are known to leap high into the air, splashing on their sides upon re-entry. Unlike the other large right whale, bowhead whales often sink when killed.

Physical description: Stockiest of all whales, with a very large head. The mouth is bowed upward more extremely than that of either of the other whales of this family. Paired nostrils are located on the rise of the forehead. Their smooth bodies are remarkably free of external parasites. The body tapers sharply along the peduncle to the flukes.

Color: Generally blue-black overall. Sloughing skin gives a mottled effect. Many individual animals display white coloration or patches randomly on the stomach region, lower jaw, and peduncle.

Fins and flukes: No dorsal fin. The flippers are small compared with the body and somewhat paddle shaped. Well-spread, well-defined flukes are pointed at the tips, with a median notch.

Length and weight: Adults reach 15 m (50 ft) and about 60,000 kg (65 tons); females are slightly larger.

Throat grooves: None.

Baleen plates: There are 325 to 360 plates on each side of upper jaw, 30 cm (12 in) wide and 4.3 m (14 ft) in length.

Feeding: Various small crustaceans, including copepods, steropods, and mysids.

Breathing and diving: Two to 6 breaths within a few minutes are followed by a longer dive averaging 15 minutes, although a dive has been known to last for up to an hour. The flukes are often raised high before a long dive, then the animal dives straight down and often returns to the point of departure. They have been reported by Eskimos to swim upside down. Two separate spouts rise 3.7 to 4.5 m (12 to 15 ft).

Mating and breeding: A 3.5 to 5.5 m (11.5 to 18 ft) calf is born after a gestation period believed to last 10 months. Calves are weaned at six months. Mating takes place during April and May, although bowheads have been observed mating in the South Chukchi Sea in mid-June. Sexual maturity is at-tained at 11.5 m (38 ft) in males, 12 m (40 ft) in females. Calving takes place at 2-year intervals.

Herding: Individuals or groups of up to 3 are found in spring; in autumn, loose groups of up to 50.

Distribution: Northern Hemisphere near the ice edge. They are indigenous to Arctic waters although their original range extended much farther south. They are currently located in four principal areas: (1) Spitzbergen, westward to east Greenland; (2) Davis Strait, Baffin Island, Hudson Bay, and adjacent waters; (3) Bering, Chukchi, Beaufort, and east Siberian seas; (4) Okhotsk Sea.

Migration: Little known. Some animals are found in Arctic waters in summer, moving south in their range as seas ice over.

Natural history notes: Lifespan may exceed 40 years.

Bruce Krogman, NMFS

Stephen Leatherwood

Above, ice has formed on the exposed back and head of this bowhead whale in the cold waters of Alaska. The characteristically rotund form and the disproportionate size of the head are clearly visible.

Left, a bowhead prepares to submerge under a vast expanse of ice. Scientists still do not understand how these whales locate their next breathing hole.

PYGMY RIGHT WHALE

Family **Balaenidae**
Genus *Caperea*
Species *C. marginata* (Gray, 1846)

Illustrated by Larry A. Foster

Although the pygmy right whale actually does not particularly resemble its larger namesake, a variety of characteristics, including the highly arched jaw, are similar to those of the other Balaenidae. Unlike the right or bowhead whales, the pygmy right whale has a dorsal fin, and from the surface this animal is often mistaken for a minke whale. For this reason, confirmed sightings of pygmy rights are very rare. The pygmy right whale is the smallest of all the great whales, and its movement when swimming is more like that of a dolphin than a great whale.

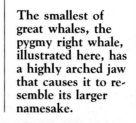

The smallest of great whales, the pygmy right whale, illustrated here, has a highly arched jaw that causes it to resemble its larger namesake.

Physical description: Stocky body with bowed lower jaw whose arch is believed to become more pronounced as the animal ages. It is this characteristic that causes them to resemble and be named after the right whale. The lower jaw projects slightly beyond the upper.

Color: Dark dorsal side which may turn increasingly darker as the animal ages. The dorsal blends into the gray-white ventral region.

Fins and flukes: A prominent falcate dorsal fin is located two-thirds of the way down the body. The flippers are small and rounded, located far under the body. Flukes are broad with a well-developed median notch.

Length and weight: Pygmy rights reach 6.1 m (20 ft) and about 4,500 kg (5 tons). Females are slightly larger.

Throat grooves: Two throat grooves correspond to the line of the lower jaw bone; these grooves may be used for feeding in a manner similar to that of such cetaceans as the gray whale and the beaked and bottlenose whales.

Baleen plates: There are 230 pairs on each side of the upper jaw, yellow-white with a white outer edge. The plates may darken with age. They reach about 69 cm (27 in) in length.

Feeding: Stomach contents of two animals contained copepods.

Breathing and diving: Limited observation confirms surfacing about every 50 seconds for about 5 minutes. Longer dives last 4 to 5 minutes. They do not raise the flukes out of the water prior to long dives. Head and lower jaw often rise out of the water when the whale surfaces. The blow is small and inconspicuous.

Mating and breeding: Little known. Newborns are thought to be about 1.5 m (4.5 ft) long.

Herding: These whales apparently live alone for the most part, although herds of up to 8 animals have been observed.

Distribution: Known only from the Southern Hemisphere. Sightings and strandings have taken place in southeastern and southwestern Australia, Tasmania, southern New Zealand, South Africa, the Falkland Islands, and the Crozet Islands in Antarctica. Also reported off Buenos Aires, Argentina.

Migration: Suggested migration corresponds with paucity or abundance of food. Juveniles of South Africa are thought to migrate to inshore waters in spring and summer.

A killer whale breaks the surface of Puget Sound with its blow.

TOOTHED WHALES
SUBORDER: ODONTOCETI

SPERM WHALES
FAMILY: PHYSETERIDAE

sperm whale
pygmy sperm whale
dwarf sperm whale

SPERM WHALES represent an early cetacean success story that has remained almost unchanged for some 30 million years or about two million sperm whale generations. They may have been the first marine mammals to exploit the food supplies of the benthos, the cold, dark realm near the bottom of the ocean where creatures bizarre to us live, along with some more familiar ones. Except for the Ziphiidae or beaked whales, sperm whales are the only cetaceans that venture to these amazing depths, 1.5 km (a mile) and more below the surface of the sea.

How they survive the enormous pressures of these dives, even how they catch their prey, remain mysteries despite our long acquaintance with these whales. They are so difficult to study in the depths of the sea that, in many respects, sperm whales might live on some other planet and be no less known than they now are. It is only when they rise to the surface, as they must do to breathe, that we see them and have the opportunity to study them at all.

We know that sperm whales produce intense, powerful clicking sounds. We assume they use these sounds to echolocate their prey and to ascertain the topography of their environment. It may be that they also use them to communicate with one another, but if so they must have little to say since the clicks are monotonously repetitive. Listening to a herd of sperm whales is a little like listening to a score of carpenters nailing up a wall.

No one knows precisely how a sperm whale produces its intense clicks. Kenneth S. Norris has put forth the intriguing theory that the gigantic spermaceti organ (a complex mass of oil-filled connective tissue and sacs occupying most of the sperm whale's forehead; the organ may be as much as 5 meters or 16 feet long and weigh several thousand kilograms) acts as a resonating chamber for thunderous claps of sound produced by air exploding through a tight constriction in the right nasal passage. The sound is then emitted in pulses that correspond to reflections off the parabola-shaped skull region behind the spermaceti organ. As in an echo-chamber, part of each reflection is rereflected from the front end of the spermaceti organ by air-filled sacs that retain and recycle the blasts of air from the nasal passage instead of exhaling them. The sound bounces back and forth in the whale's head producing diminishing replicas of the initial sound. This theory seems to agree with facts regarding the whale's anatomy and the nature of the pulsed clicks. But no one has yet rigged up a sperm whale to test its intricate workings, and it is hardly likely that anyone ever will, at least with a healthy, free-living sperm whale—they are tremendously strong animals.

The sperm whale possesses the largest brain of any creature that has ever lived on earth, but no one knows what it does with so much neocortical tissue. As the long and successful reign of the dinosaurs shows us, the brain need not be oversized to control the motor functions of even a large animal; indeed, control of the motor functions seems to occupy only a small part of the whale's brain, while the rest of it is highly developed, much as the human brain.

Theories and myths concerning its large brain often credit the sperm whale with the power of cognition and perhaps even extreme intelligence, but no one is sure how to find out what goes on in there. Some investigators suggest that the sperm whale's brain creates a sort of acoustic hologram from the echoes of all those clicks, and from the other sounds in the animal's environment—that the sperm whale "pictures" with its ears as we do with our eyes. It would require great computational faculties to accomplish this feat, but, considering the sophisticated awareness of their surroundings that the sperm whales' dolphin cousins seem to

acquire through echolocation with their smaller brains, we cannot rule out the possibility.

Aggressive encounters between humans and sperm whales were frequent in centuries past, and often meant disaster for the land-based mammal. Whaling literature is replete with tales of ships stove in, whaleboats and whalers smashed to bits by furiously snapping jaws, the bits flailed to oblivion by powerful flukes that turned the water white. The hazards of small-boat encounters with sperm whales on the high seas still remain today.

In its evolution toward deep diving, the sperm whale has lost its adaptation for shallow water. Entire herds of sperm whales occasionally become disoriented close to shore and strand. This phenomenon is common among a number of species of cetaceans and is poorly understood. In some parts of the world, mass strandings of sperm whales have taken place repeatedly, leading to the theory that

A sperm whale breaches in the eastern tropical Pacific. Scientists believe that the swollen throat of this animal is caused by the whale's tongue, pushed out by gravity and the momentum of the leap.

near-shore bottom topography in those areas may confuse the whales. Advocates of another theory contend that parasitical infestations of the whales' ears may confuse their acoustical senses, leading to the strandings.

Among the sperm whales there are two diminutive forms known as the pygmy and dwarf sperm whales. Both animals resemble their giant namesake in many ways, including the possession of a spermaceti organ; but because they are not so numerous as the larger sperm whale, have virtually no commercial value, and are, therefore, not hunted, our knowledge of them comes primarily from examination of stranded specimens.

SPERM WHALE

cachalot

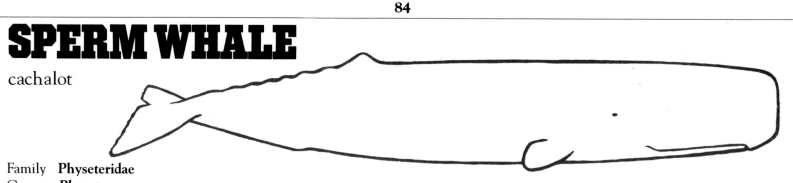

Family **Physeteridae**
Genus *Physeter*
Species *P. macrocephalus*   Linnaeus, 1758

Taxonomic note: *Physeter catodon* is often used although *Physeter macrocephalus* now takes precedence.

When most people think of a whale, the sperm whale is the animal that comes to mind, mostly because of the great white sperm whale, Moby Dick, in Herman Melville's classic novel of that name. They are the most numerous of the great whales and were the basis of the success of very early American whaling operations. Sperm whales have a huge, squarish forehead, small, inconspicuous eyes, and a very small thin lower jaw which fits into the large head. The forehead contains the spermaceti organ, a name given to it by early whalers who believed this organ contained sperm. Actually, the organ contains a high quality oil that when removed from the body and cooled takes on a waxy quality. Kenneth S. Norris, of the University of California at Santa Cruz, has recently proposed that the sperm whale may use the spermaceti organ to produce noises so loud that they stun the whale's prey.

The disproportionately small eyes of the sperm whale probably do not play a large role in the daily activities of the animal. These whales often feed at such great depths (over 900 m or 3,000 ft) that eyes must prove of little value in their quest for food.

The lower jaw of the male sperm whale reaches 4.5 m (15 ft) in length and contains up to 50 of the most massive teeth on earth. The upper jaw contains no visible teeth, and it is a wonder how these animals prove so formidable in their pursuit of giant squid, the mainstay of their diet.

While they are found in all oceans—almost exclusively in deep water—their distribution is regulated by habit and migration. During the latter the populations separate by age and sex. In summer, most of the adolescent and mature males form "bachelor pods" and migrate to the cold nutrient-rich waters of the high latitudes, while the females and young animals form "nursing pods" and remain in temperate waters.

Physical description: The skin is rippled over much of the body, especially on the back and sides. The body shape is unique among cetaceans, with a squared head region constituting about one-third of the total body length. The sperm whale has a single blowhole, located on the left side of the slope of the forehead. About one of every 200 sperm whales has a deformed lower jaw which does not seem to interfere with feeding.

Color: Light brown to blue-gray, often with distinctly lighter shading around the belly and jaw. Lips are marbled outside the white mouth.

Fins and flukes: In place of a dorsal fin, a series of bumps, often including a single large triangular bump, extends along the ridge of the spine from midback almost to tail. Small, stubby flippers are located well to the rear of the eyes—themselves located just above the convergence of the upper and lower jaws. Small, broad, thin flukes have rounded tips and a definite median notch. The flukes are often disfigured or serrated along their trailing edges.

Length and weight: Males reach 18.5 m (60 ft) and weigh about 32,000 to 45,000 kg (35 to 50 tons); females reach 13 m (43 ft) and 16,000 kg (18 tons).

Teeth: The 18 to 25 large, conical teeth in each side of the lower jaw fit into sockets in the upper jaw. The 10 to 16 teeth in the upper jaw rarely erupt through gums.

Feeding: Squid is the primary food.

Breathing and diving: This whale can dive to depths of at least 1,000 m (3,300 ft) and can remain underwater for over an hour. Prior to a lengthy dive a sperm whale may remain on the surface for about 10 minutes, blowing every 10 to 30 seconds, then raise its flukes high out of the water and submerge. The blow is forward and to the left.

Mating and breeding: A 3.7 to 4.3 m (12 to 14 ft) calf weighing 900 kg (1 ton) is born after a gestation period of 16 months. Lactation lasts up to 24 months. Males attain sexual maturity at about 10 years or more; females at 8 to 11 years. Physical maturity is reached at about 24 to 25 years.

Herding: Groups of 3 to 40 are seen, sometimes spread out over many miles. Solitary bulls are often sighted.

Distribution: All oceans except polar ice fields.

Courtesy The Cousteau Society

Migration: It has been suggested that migrations are dependent on water temperatures, abundance of cephalopods, and presence or absence of harem herds. Only the Atlantic and Pacific migrations are understood. In the Atlantic herds range as far south as Venezuela in winter; as far north as Davis Strait in summer, but avoid polar ice packs; females and juveniles remain between 30° and 50° north latitude, while adult males range farther north. Pacific herds winter off the slopes of continental California as far south as Baja California, the Gulf of California, and the Clipperton Islands; in summer they migrate past the Aleutians as far north as the Bering Sea.

Natural history notes: Sperm whales are generally believed to live as long as 70 years.

A rare underwater photograph of a sperm whale calf in the Indian Ocean. Note the characteristically blunt head and barely discernible flippers.

Robert Pitman

Bill Rossiter

Above, a sperm whale breaches in the eastern tropical Pacific Ocean.

Right, discovered trying to beach itself off Fire Island, New York, in 1981, this sperm whale was towed into a boat basin, nursed back to health and released, a first in the history of cetacean rescue attempts.

PYGMY SPERM WHALE

Family **Physeteridae**
Genus *Kogia*
Species ***K. breviceps***   (de Blainville, 1838)

The pygmy sperm whale is one of three members of the family Physeteridae and has certain basic similarities to the sperm whale. Both have an underslung, small lower jaw containing the only functional teeth, an asymetrical blowhole placed slightly to the left of the forehead, a spermaceti organ, and many skeletal similarities. Also, like the sperm whale, pygmy sperm whales are not coastal animals; indeed, their deep sea distribution and the fact that they were never the prey of industrial whalers makes them very little known. They are slow and deliberate swimmers and can easily be approached by boats when encountered at sea. Most of what we know about this species comes from animals which have washed up on shore alive and been taken to marine parks for observation. None has survived more than a couple of weeks in captivity. The pygmy sperm and the dwarf sperm whale formerly were considered a single species.

Physical description: This whale has a very stocky body. The head is squared with the lower jaw hinged well behind the snout. A single blowhole is located slightly to the left of the forehead. The caudal peduncle tapers abruptly to the flukes.

Color: The dark brown-black dorsal side gradually fades to light ventral flanks. Behind the eyes a dark patch resembling a fish's gill cover extends the height of the head region.

Fins and flukes: A tiny falcate dorsal fin is located to the rear of the midback region. Flippers are large and slightly rounded at tips with straight leading edges and convex trailing edges. Flukes are large and slightly rounded at tips, with a definite median notch.

Length and weight: Pygmy sperm whales reach 3.4 m (11 ft) and may exceed 400 kg (900 lbs).

Teeth: There are 10 to 16 long, curved, needle-sharp teeth in each side of the lower jaw, fitting into sockets in the upper jaw. No teeth in upper jaw.

Feeding: These whales feed mostly on octopus and squid, but also take small fish, crabs and other invertebrates.

Breathing and diving: Rises slowly to the surface to breathe, blows inconspicuously. Does not roll forward at surface as do most small whales.

Mating and breeding: Calves, 1.2 m (4 ft), are thought to be born in late spring after an 11-month gestation. Males are sexually mature at 2.7 to 3 m (9 to 9.75 ft), females at 2.6 to 2.7 m (8.5 to 9 ft).

Herding: Individually, or groups of 2 to 3.

Distribution: Worldwide in tropical and warm temperate waters.

Migration: No information is available.

Natural history notes: This is a very shy animal that will not itself approach boats, but on calm days a boat can approach closely as the animals lie quietly on the surface looking very much like logs with dorsal fins.

DWARF SPERM WHALE

Family **Physeteridae**
Genus ***Kogia***
Species ***K. simus***   Owen, 1866

The dwarf sperm whale is smaller than the pygmy sperm whale and exhibits several distinguishing features. The falcate dorsal fin is tall, prominent, and located on the midback region. There is a gill-shaped color pattern behind the eyes as with the pygmy sperm whale. The dwarf sperm has, however, fewer teeth and two parallel creases under the throat which are not present in the pygmy sperm. It is a very rare animal insofar as confirmed sightings are concerned, and most information comes from infrequent strandings.

Physical description: Stocky body. A single blowhole is located slightly to the left of the forehead. Several short, irregular throat grooves resemble those found among beaked whales.

Color: Dark dorsal side converges to lighter flanks and ventral side with a dark, gill-shaped coloration behind each eye.

Fins and flukes: High, prominent, falcate dorsal fin located on the midback region. Flippers are rounded at the tips. Flukes are well developed, slightly rounded at the tips, with a definite median notch.

Length and weight: The dwarf sperm whale reaches 2.1 to 2.7 m (6.75 to 8.75 ft) and 135 to 275 kg (300 to 600 lbs).

Teeth: 7 to 13 sharply pointed, backward-curved teeth are found in each side of the lower jaw, fitting into sockets in the upper jaw. Usually there are 1 to 3 rudimentary teeth in each side of the upper jaw.

Feeding: Mostly squid, but fish and crustaceans also are eaten.

Breathing and diving: These animals are known to dive to at least 300 m (1,000 ft). The blow is inconspicuous, and the animal presents less of the body when "logging" on the surface than its cousin the pygmy sperm whale.

Mating and breeding: Length at birth is about 1 m (3.3 ft) and calves nurse until more than 1.5 m (5 ft) in length. The gestation period is about 11 months. Females may give birth in successive years.

Herding: Often seen individually, or in groups of less than 10. There may be some segregation by age and sex, similar to that among sperm whales (page 84).

Distribution: The seas adjacent to South Africa, India, Sri Lanka, Japan, Hawaii, Baja California, California, and the eastern United States.

Migration: No information is available.

While dwarf and pygmy sperm whales are much smaller than their giant cousin, the sperm whale, and have a dorsal fin, which the sperm whale does not, all three species share a blunt head; narrow, underslung jaw; asymmetrical placement of the blowhole; and many skeletal similarities.

William H. Dawbin

Only recently have scientists been able to identify differences between pygmy and dwarf sperm whales, in the past considered the same animal. Beached and later brought to Marineland of Florida, this dwarf sperm whale exhibits its characteristic dorsal fin, much larger and farther forward than the fin of the pygmy sperm.

Marineland of Florida

An underwater photograph of a dwarf sperm whale shows the underslung jaw and the gill-like color pattern behind the eyes.

BEAKED AND BOTTLENOSE WHALES
FAMILY: ZIPHIIDAE
(formerly Hyperoodontidae)

Baird's beaked whale	Longman's beaked whale	Hubbs' beaked whale
Arnoux's beaked whale	Hector's beaked whale	Stejneger's beaked whale
Cuvier's beaked whale	True's beaked whale	Andrews' beaked whale
Shepherd's beaked whale	Gervais' beaked whale	Sowerby's beaked whale
northern bottlenose whale	ginkgo-toothed whale	strap-toothed whale
southern bottlenose whale	Gray's beaked whale	Blainville's beaked whale

THE ANCESTORS of these cetaceans appeared about 30 million years ago and flourished during the Miocene epoch, 25 to 10 million years ago. At that time they developed into dozens of species some of whose descendents survive today.

The beaked and bottlenose whales are generally shy creatures inhabiting remote offshore waters. Several species have not been described sufficiently to be recognized at sea. Most of the information about these whales has been collected by beachcombing for carcasses washed ashore by circumstance rather than by whaling research or marine surveys. Relatively few specimens have been collected for study and some of the ziphiids are very little known—unknown species may exist yet.

The excitement of exploring the unknown has attracted many serious cetologists to the study of Ziphiidae at one time or other. All cetologists are beachcombers at heart and hope that someday they will chance upon a creature no one else has ever seen or will have the opportunity to describe a specimen of one of the world's rarest whales. Because the ziphiids are so rare and so rarely seen, a beginner can make his name in the field almost overnight, and a specialist has few peers. Yet the mysteries these strange whales present will not be easily solved by the handful of specimens chance provides in one lifetime. More than any other group of mammals, ziphiids offer an opportunity for biological sleuthing that will be available for several more human generations. (Unfortunately, it is illegal for citizens to beachcomb for whale remains in the United States without a federal permit. The pursuit of knowledge is not thereby served,

and an important and exciting avenue of research for fledgling cetologists is closed.)

While it is true that more is unknown than is known about the Ziphiidae, some facts will be given in the species summaries that follow. In general, beaked and bottlenose whales are characterized by wishbone-shaped indentations or grooves on their throats and few—usually two—teeth. The dorsal fin is typically falcate and located about two-thirds of the body length from the beak, and the flukes usually lack a median notch. All are pelagic and presumably can dive to great depths. Those species whose diets are known prey predominantly on oceanic squid and fish dwelling at moderate to considerable depths. While the smallest ziphiids may reach only about 3.7 m (12 ft) at maturity, the largest may exceed 12 m (40 ft). Most are extensively scarred and scratched, suggesting that they lead aggressive if not pugnacious lives.

This remarkable photograph is the only one known of a Blainville's beaked whale mother and calf.

BAIRD'S BEAKED WHALE

northern giant bottlenose whale

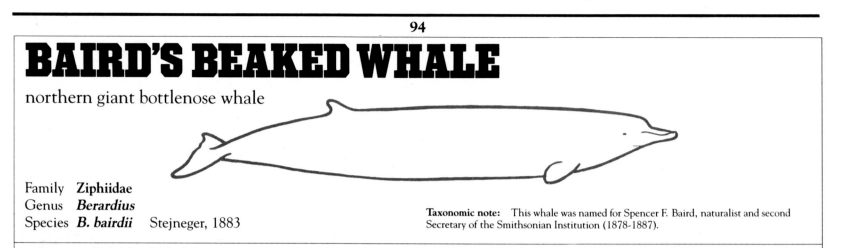

Family **Ziphiidae**
Genus **Berardius**
Species **B. bairdii**   Stejneger, 1883

Taxonomic note: This whale was named for Spencer F. Baird, naturalist and second Secretary of the Smithsonian Institution (1878-1887).

Baird's beaked whales are very gregarious animals, often found in large groups of 30 or more. They and Arnoux's beaked whale (page 98) may well represent different populations of the same species; only through comparison of specimens can this be confirmed or disproven. Baird's beaked whales are deep divers, frequenting areas of the North Pacific around escarpments and seamounts. They are shy in areas where they have been hunted, but elsewhere may be inquisitive about ships and may be approached closely.

Illustrated by Larry A. Foster

Left, limited to the north Pacific, the Baird's beaked whale is a gregarious animal, though the scar marks, evident in this illustration, indicate intraspecies fighting.

Physical description: The body is cigar shaped with a thin rostrum and significantly protruding lower jaw. The rostrum meets a high, rising, well-developed bulbous forehead. The flippers, flukes, and forehead may be somewhat larger than those of its southern counterpart.

Color: Dark blue dorsally, light gray ventrally, mottled on the flanks.

Fins and flukes: Small triangular or falcate dorsal fin is located well to the rear of the midback region. Flippers are small, paddle shaped, and rounded at the tips, located higher up on the sides than in most other cetaceans. Flukes are large, somewhat rounded at the tips, and seldom possess a median notch.

Length and weight: Largest recorded male was 11.9 m (39 ft) long; the largest recorded female 12.8 m (42 ft). They are estimated to exceed 11,000 kg (12 tons).

Teeth: Two pairs of erupted teeth are in the lower jaw; a triangular pair, about fist size, protrudes visibly from the tip of the lower jaw. The thumb-sized second pair is located farther back, concealed in the mouth and separated from the first pair by a considerable space.

Feeding: They are known to feed on squid and small fish.

Breathing and diving: Both forms of *Berardius* can dive to depths of 1,000 m (3,300 ft). The dive may last from 20 minutes to 1 hour.

Mating and breeding: Calves 4.5 m (15 ft) in length are thought to be born between late November and early May after a gestation period estimated between 12 and 17 months. Males may attain sexual maturity at about 10 to 11 m (32 to 36 ft); no data are available on females. Calving probably takes place at 3-year intervals. Birthing is thought to occur near the Japanese archipelago, among other possible places.

Kenneth C. Balcomb, III

Herding: Normally these whales congregate in groups of about 6, but herds of up to 40 or more, led by a large male, have been reported.

Distribution: They are found in the North Pacific from Japan and southern California northward to the Bering Sea.

Migration: These animals apparently have a northward movement in their range during the summer months, and a southward movement in winter.

Natural history notes: There is much scarring visible on the body, doubtless from intraspecies fighting. The lifespan is estimated at more than 70 years. This species became known to western science from a skull obtained from Bering Island in 1881. Two years earlier a portion of a skull of the same species was found on Bering Island, but its description was not published until a few months after that of Stejneger's.

Above, a Baird's beaked whale swims off Tokyo Bay. Both sexes of this species have a pair of large teeth at the tip of the jaw and a smaller pair just behind.

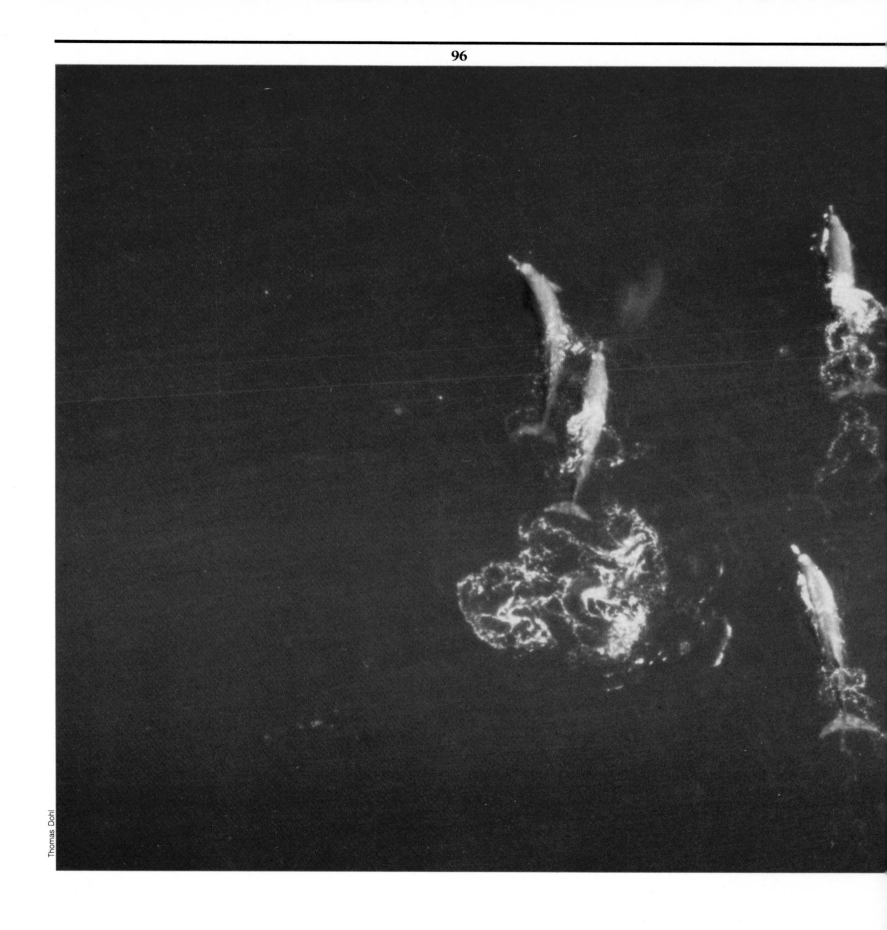

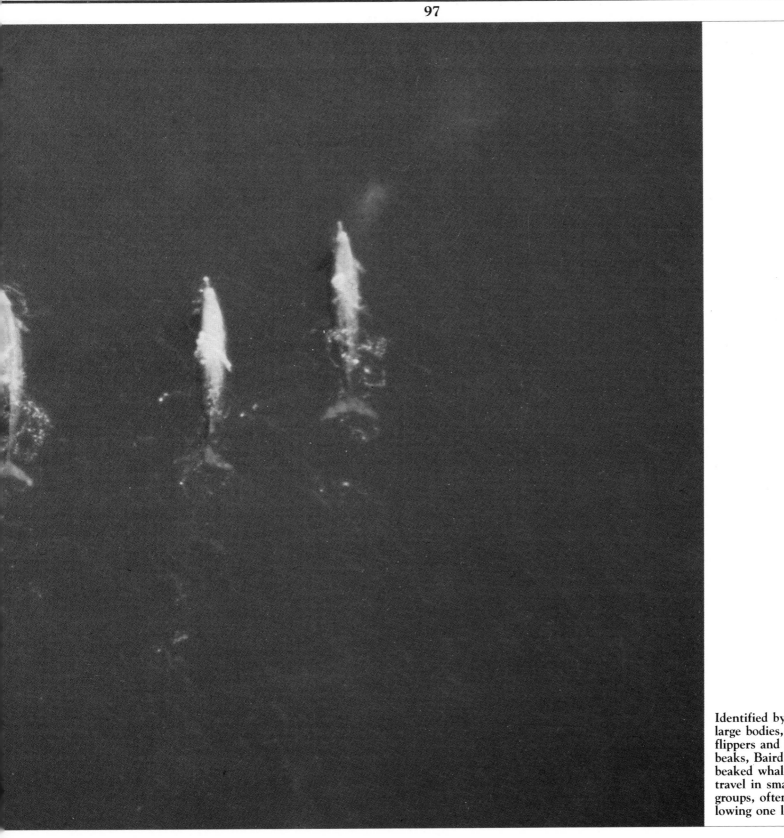

Identified by their large bodies, slight flippers and long beaks, Baird's beaked whales travel in small groups, often following one leader.

ARNOUX'S BEAKED WHALE

southern giant bottlenose whale

Family **Ziphiidae**
Genus **Berardius**
Species **B. arnuxii**   Duvernoy, 1851

Much less well known than its northern counterpart, Arnoux's beaked whale occurs near deep escarpments and seamounts of the Southern Hemisphere, particularly around New Zealand and Australia. It is known mostly from specimens and photographs of beached or stranded animals, and its habits and behavior are presumed to be similar to the Baird's beaked whale. The distribution of the two species suggests that their populations have been separated since the last ice age.

Physical description: The cigar-shaped body has a thin rostrum and protruding lower jaw. The rostrum meets a high, rising, well-developed bulbous forehead.

Color: Black or dark gray with many long white scars thought to result from mating fights, giving the body a light overall appearance. Flanks and ventral regions are lighter than the dorsal area.

Fins and flukes: Small triangular or falcate dorsal fin is located well to the rear of the midback region. Flippers are small, paddle shaped, and rounded at the tips, located closer to the chin than those of most other whales. Flukes are large and somewhat rounded at the tips, seldom possessing a median notch.

Length and weight: These whales reach about 9 m (30 ft) and weigh about 8,200 kg (9 tons).

Teeth: Two pairs of erupted teeth in lower jaw; a triangular pair about fist sized protrudes from the tip of the lower jaw; a second, thumb-sized pair located about 20 cm (8 in) back is concealed inside the mouth.

Feeding: Squid and bottom-dwelling fish.

Breathing and diving: This whale can dive to at least 1,000 m (3,300 ft); the dive may last from 20 minutes to 1 hour.

Mating and breeding: Breeding occurs in the South Atlantic and the New Zealand archipelagoes from December through March. Gestation period is 10 months.

Herding: A breeding herd may be dominated by a single bull.

Distribution: Confined to southern oceans; known from South Australia, New Zealand, Argentina, Falkland Islands, South Georgia, South Shetlands, South Africa, and Antarctic Peninsula.

Migration: Presumed to migrate seasonally away from the edge of the ice in winter for breeding, although some have been known to become trapped by shifting ice around Antarctica, and may winter or die there.

Natural history notes: This species became known to science as a result of a specimen that stranded in Akoroa Harbor, Banks Peninsula, New Zealand, and was presented to the Museum of Paris in 1846 by one M. Arnoux, surgeon to the French corvette *Rhin*, commanded by a Captain Bérard.

Frank Robson

Above, this apparently healthy Arnoux's beaked whale attempted to strand itself in Hawkes Bay, New Zealand. A patient cetologist spent many hours guiding it back to sea.

Right, an Arnoux's beaked whale swims near a southern New Zealand beach. The bulbous forehead and the crescent-shaped, forward-facing blowhole are typical of the *Berardius* genus to which this whale belongs.

Frank Robson

SHEPHERD'S BEAKED WHALE

Tasman beaked whale

Family **Ziphiidae**
Genus **Tasmacetus**
Species **T. shepherdi**   Oliver, 1937

Cetologist William A. Watkins recently reported the first probable sighting of a Shepherd's beaked whale off New Zealand. It was not described until 1937 and remains one of the least known of all cetaceans. Most information has been derived from limited strandings in New Zealand, Argentina, and Chile. The animal has been assigned its own genus because, among other things, it is the only beaked whale with functional dolphinlike rows of teeth in both the upper and lower jaws.

Illustrated by Larry A. Foster

Physical description: This large stocky animal resembles a cross between a bottlenose whale (page 102) and a typical beaked whale. Its circumference nearly equals its length. Typical beaked-whale wishbone throat indentations are found.

Color: Dark brown dorsal becomes lighter on sides, white ventrally.

Fins and flukes: Well-developed falcate dorsal fin is located slightly to the rear of the midback region; it is larger than those of other beaked whales. Flippers are small, and the flukes display little or no median notch.

Length and weight: Males reach a recorded length of 7 m (23 ft); females may reach equal size or larger, but the greatest recorded length was 6.6 m (22 ft).

Teeth: 17 to 19 teeth are located in each side of the upper jaw, and 23 to 28 teeth in each side of the lower, including a pair of very large teeth at the tip, which do not erupt in females.

Feeding: Stomach samples from one stranded animal confirmed feeding on bottom fish.

Breathing and diving: No information is available.

Mating and breeding: No information is available.

Herding: No information is available.

Distribution: Known from limited strandings in New Zealand, Argentina, and Chile, suggesting a Southern Hemisphere distribution.

Migration: No information is available.

Shepherd's beaked whale, illustrated here, is one of the least known of all cetaceans, distinguished from other beaked whales by functional, dolphinlike rows of teeth on both upper and lower jaws.

CUVIER'S BEAKED WHALE

goose beaked whale

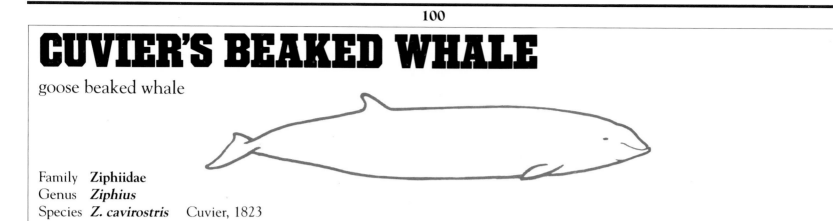

Family **Ziphiidae**
Genus **Ziphius**
Species **Z. cavirostris**   Cuvier, 1823

Cuvier's beaked whales are the most common "rare" whales. Scientific specimens are known mostly from strandings throughout their world-wide range. Sightings of this species are infrequent as the blow is inconspicuous and the animals normally show little interest in ships.

This photograph of a breaching Cuvier's beaked whale dispelled the notion that beaked and bottlenose whales never leap out of the water.

Physical description: Well-defined indentation on the dorsal region just behind the head. The cleft of the mouth is smaller than that of any other beaked whale, and the beak is indistinct in larger individuals. Typical wishbone indentations are found on the ventral region of the chin.

Color: Rusty red-brown dorsally, converging to darker brown on flanks; dark brown or black ventrally. Forehead, chin, and mouth are white on older animals. Old males display a distinctly white head. The entire body, especially the ventral region, is covered with small white blotches caused by parasitic bacteria or protozoa. Most individuals are visibly scarred, probably from fights with older, aggressive males.

Fins and flukes: The falcate dorsal fin is usually tall—up to 38 cm (15 in), and taller in Atlantic and Pacific animals than those of the Indian Ocean—and is located to the rear of the midback region. Flippers are small and rounded at the tips with straight leading edges; the back edges curve to meet the body. Large, well-defined flukes are rounded at the tips; they may or may not have a median notch.

Length and weight: Cuvier's beaked whales may reach about 7 m (23 ft) and exceed 4,500 kg (5 tons). Females are slightly larger than males of the same age.

Teeth: A pair of teeth is located at the tip of the lower jaw in males. These teeth do not erupt visibly in females.

Feeding: Squid and deep-dwelling oceanic fish are known to be consumed.

Breathing and diving: These are deep-diving animals, able to remain underwater as long as half an hour. Prior to lengthy dives, they breathe 2 or 3 times at 10- to 20-second intervals, often raising their flukes high into the air at a 45-degree angle, then descending vertically. Blows are neither large nor obvious; the forehead, back, and dorsal fin are visible, but usually not the beak. These animals rarely breach and are wary of boats.

Mating and breeding: Calves are born between 2 and 3 m (6.5 and 10 ft). Males are sexually mature at 5.5 m (18 ft); females at 6 m (20 ft).

Herding: The average herd size is believed to be from 2 to 6.

Distribution: These are cosmopolitan animals found in all oceans and seas except in the polar regions. They typically occur in waters of 1,000 m (3,300 ft) or deeper, often in the vicinity of sea canyons and escarpments.

Migration: No information is available.

Natural history notes: They are thought to live at least 35 years.

Stephen Leatherwood

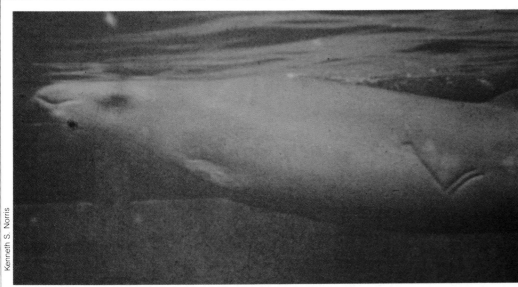

Kenneth S. Norris

Left, found stranded in the surf line of southern California this Cuvier's beaked whale was taken to Marineland of the Pacific. The scar is believed to be a partially healed shark bite.

Below, this Cuvier's beaked whale was one of a pod of six individuals that entered the port of Baltra in the Galapagos Islands and attempted to beach themselves. Five survived, finally swimming back to sea.

Heinrich Schatz, Courtesy Gary Robinson

NORTHERN BOTTLENOSE WHALE

Family **Ziphiidae**
Genus **Hyperoodon**
Species **H. ampullatus** (Forster, 1770)

As with several other varieties of cetacean, the northern bottlenose whale has a counterpart in the Southern Hemisphere which, but for subtle differences, appears to be an identical animal. They may very well be conspecifics divided into northern and southern populations since the last ice age (see southern bottlenose whale, page 103).

Northern bottlenose whales have been hunted for hundreds of years. They are extremely protective of other members of the herd, a trait the whalers found useful. Wounding one animal would bring others within harpoon range so that the entire herd could be taken.

The bottlenose whale is characterized by an abrupt, rounded forehead, or melon, the primary function of which is believed to be echolocation.

Physical description: A bulbous forehead, more pronounced in males than in females, grows as the animal ages; the rostrum is well developed. The body is long and comparatively thin; the eyes are very small.

Color: Juveniles are completely dark brown to black, becoming lighter as they age. Very old animals are white with gray-white patches covering the dorsal and flank regions. Flippers and flukes remain brown and are always darker on both sides than the darkest body color.

Fins and flukes: The pointed, falcate dorsal fin, located well to the rear of the midback region, is extremely well developed and may reach 38 cm (15 in) in height. Flippers are small and pointed at their tips. Flukes are wide and somewhat pointed, with no median notch.

Length and weight: Males reach a known length of 9.8 m (32 ft); females are slightly smaller.

Teeth: One pair of teeth is located in the tip of the lower jaw: they may not erupt even in mature animals, and they may fall out in older ones. Sometimes a second pair is located behind the first. There are no teeth in the upper jaw. Teeth do not erupt in females.

Feeding: Squid is the primary food.

Breathing and diving: These animals remain on the surface breathing for about 10 minutes prior to a lengthy dive. The blow, about 1.8 m (6 ft) tall, is visible for about 90 m (300 ft).

Mating and breeding: Mating is thought to take place in the spring with 3 m (10 ft) calves born after a gestation period of 12 months. Calving interval is 2 to 3 years. Males are sexually mature at about 7.3 m (24 ft); females at 6.7 to 7 m (22 to 23 ft).

Herding: The average is 10 to 15 animals, but sometimes herds number as many as 25.

Distribution: North Atlantic from Davis Strait and Novaya Zemlya, southwest to Rhode Island and the English Channel.

Migration: North in spring; south to the Azores and Mediterranean Sea in July.

Natural history notes: These are very inquisitive animals and accounts of them approaching boats are not unusual.

Illustrated by Larry A. Foster

This illustration of a bottlenose whale reveals the characteristically bulbous forehead, or melon, that is believed to play a role in echolocation.

SOUTHERN BOTTLENOSE WHALE

Family **Ziphiidae**
Genus **Hyperoodon**
Species **H. planifrons**   Flower, 1882

L iving mainly in the southern oceans, far from shipping lanes, the southern bottlenose whale, unlike its northern counterpart, is rarely observed in the wild. It has never been subjected to systematic whaling, and is known only from about a dozen specimens.

Physical description: Practically identical to the northern bottlenose whale (page 102) except possibly slightly smaller, with a more bulbous forehead and larger, more prominent dorsal fin. The forehead has a slight flat spot at the anterior ridge.

Color: Similar to northern bottlenose.

Length and weight: Males reach a known length of 9.8 m (32 ft); females reach about 7.5 m (24.5 ft).

Teeth: A single pair of prominent teeth projects from the tip of the male's lower jaw. No teeth are present in the upper jaw. Teeth do not erupt through the gums in females.

Feeding: Known to feed on squid.

Breathing and diving: Like the northern bottlenose, this animal's blow rises about 1.8 m (6 ft). They are deep divers and may stay down for an hour.

Mating and breeding: No information available.

Herding: Herds apparently are small—2 to 12.

Distribution: Southern oceans; known from Australia, the Falkland Islands, South Georgia, the South Orkney Islands, South Africa, and off the coast of Antarctica in the Pacific and Indian Ocean sectors.

Migration: North toward tropics in winter; south in summer.

LONGMAN'S BEAKED WHALE

Indo-Pacific beaked whale

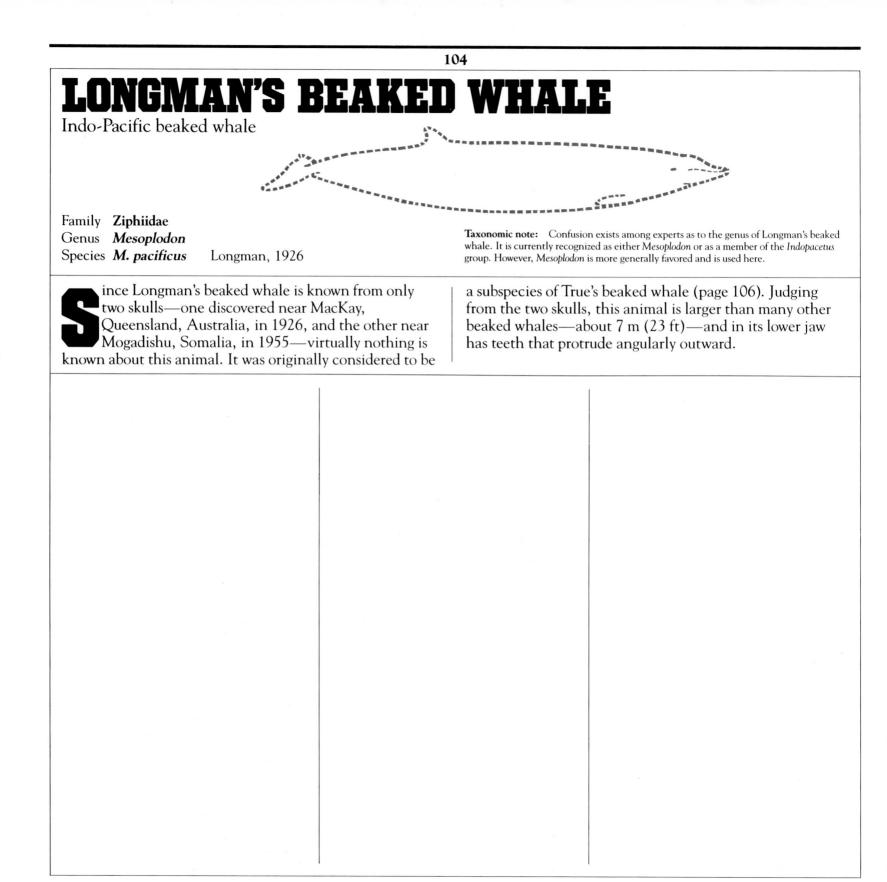

Family **Ziphiidae**
Genus **Mesoplodon**
Species **M. pacificus**   Longman, 1926

Taxonomic note: Confusion exists among experts as to the genus of Longman's beaked whale. It is currently recognized as either *Mesoplodon* or as a member of the *Indopacetus* group. However, *Mesoplodon* is more generally favored and is used here.

Since Longman's beaked whale is known from only two skulls—one discovered near MacKay, Queensland, Australia, in 1926, and the other near Mogadishu, Somalia, in 1955—virtually nothing is known about this animal. It was originally considered to be a subspecies of True's beaked whale (page 106). Judging from the two skulls, this animal is larger than many other beaked whales—about 7 m (23 ft)—and in its lower jaw has teeth that protrude angularly outward.

HECTOR'S BEAKED WHALE

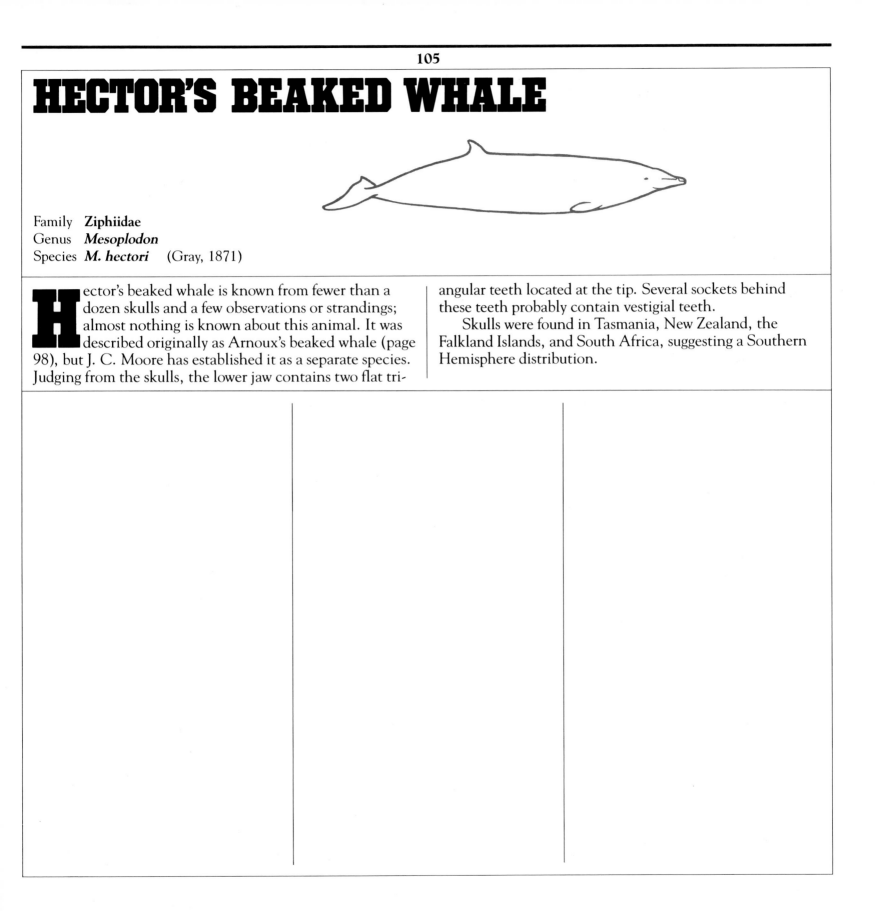

Family **Ziphiidae**
Genus *Mesoplodon*
Species *M. hectori*   (Gray, 1871)

Hector's beaked whale is known from fewer than a dozen skulls and a few observations or strandings; almost nothing is known about this animal. It was described originally as Arnoux's beaked whale (page 98), but J. C. Moore has established it as a separate species. Judging from the skulls, the lower jaw contains two flat tri-angular teeth located at the tip. Several sockets behind these teeth probably contain vestigial teeth.

Skulls were found in Tasmania, New Zealand, the Falkland Islands, and South Africa, suggesting a Southern Hemisphere distribution.

TRUE'S BEAKED WHALE

Family **Ziphiidae**
Genus **Mesoplodon**
Species **M. mirus**   True, 1913

True's beaked whale is another very rare and little-known animal. There has never been a confirmed observation at sea; the species is known from limited strandings, on the basis of which it has been seen to resemble closely Cuvier's beaked whale (page 100).

Physical description: The midbody is stocky but tapers sharply to the flukes. A very well-developed beak projects from the slightly bulbous forehead. Typical wishbone indentations are present on the throat.

Color: Dark gray or dull black dorsally, lighter gray on flanks, white on ventral region. The body may be covered with pink, yellow, or purple spots or scratches—probably tooth marks from others of this species.

Fins and flukes: The small, falcate dorsal fin is located on the extreme rear of the midback region, followed by pronounced ridges to the flukes. Very small flippers are located well up on the sides. Well-spread flukes are concave and rounded at their tips, with slight or no median notch.

Length and weight: Reaches at least 5.2 m (17 ft).

Teeth: One pair of teeth is located on the tip of the lower jaw. No teeth are found in the upper jaw. Teeth do not erupt through the gums in females.

Feeding: Various species of squid.

Breathing and diving: No information is available.

Mating and breeding: Very little is known. A 2.2 m (7 ft) calf was found with a 5.2 m (17 ft) mother during the month of March.

Herding: No information is available.

Distribution: North Atlantic from Florida and Nova Scotia east to the British Isles; an apparently isolated population exists in temperate waters off South Africa, extending possibly into the southwestern Indian Ocean.

Migration: No information is available.

GERVAIS' BEAKED WHALE

Gulf Stream beaked whale

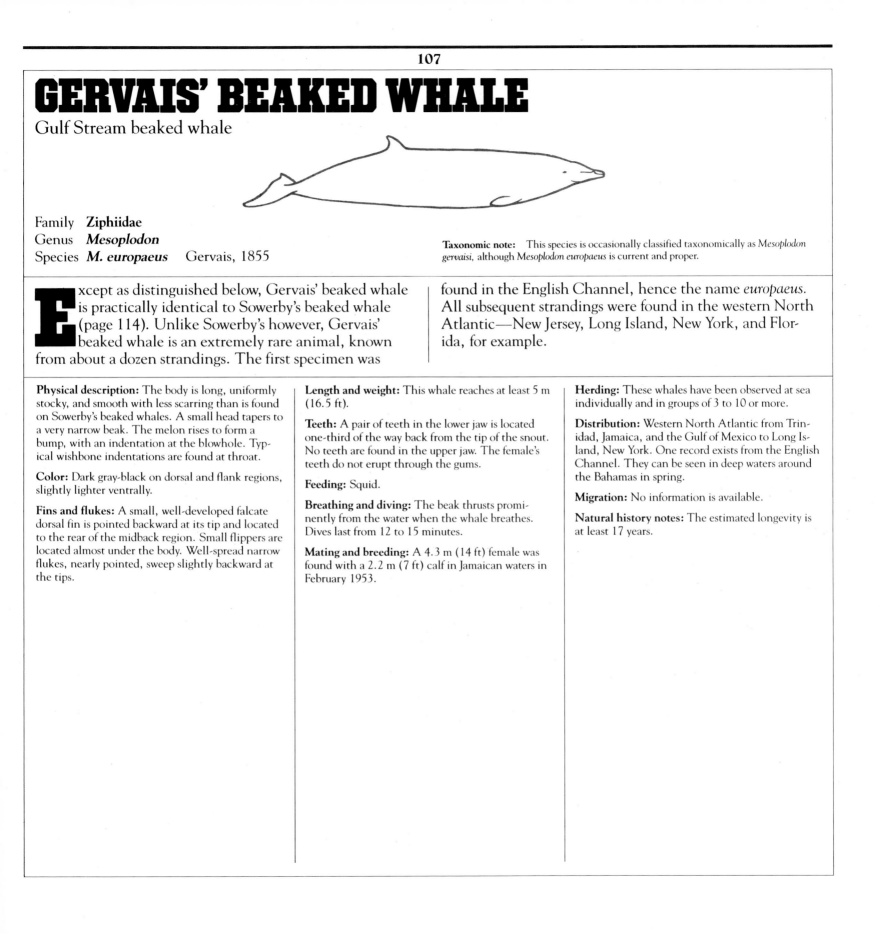

Family **Ziphiidae**
Genus **Mesoplodon**
Species **M. europaeus**   Gervais, 1855

Taxonomic note: This species is occasionally classified taxonomically as *Mesoplodon gervaisi,* although *Mesoplodon europaeus* is current and proper.

Except as distinguished below, Gervais' beaked whale is practically identical to Sowerby's beaked whale (page 114). Unlike Sowerby's however, Gervais' beaked whale is an extremely rare animal, known from about a dozen strandings. The first specimen was found in the English Channel, hence the name *europaeus.* All subsequent strandings were found in the western North Atlantic—New Jersey, Long Island, New York, and Florida, for example.

Physical description: The body is long, uniformly stocky, and smooth with less scarring than is found on Sowerby's beaked whales. A small head tapers to a very narrow beak. The melon rises to form a bump, with an indentation at the blowhole. Typical wishbone indentations are found at throat.

Color: Dark gray-black on dorsal and flank regions, slightly lighter ventrally.

Fins and flukes: A small, well-developed falcate dorsal fin is pointed backward at its tip and located to the rear of the midback region. Small flippers are located almost under the body. Well-spread narrow flukes, nearly pointed, sweep slightly backward at the tips.

Length and weight: This whale reaches at least 5 m (16.5 ft).

Teeth: A pair of teeth in the lower jaw is located one-third of the way back from the tip of the snout. No teeth are found in the upper jaw. The female's teeth do not erupt through the gums.

Feeding: Squid.

Breathing and diving: The beak thrusts prominently from the water when the whale breathes. Dives last from 12 to 15 minutes.

Mating and breeding: A 4.3 m (14 ft) female was found with a 2.2 m (7 ft) calf in Jamaican waters in February 1953.

Herding: These whales have been observed at sea individually and in groups of 3 to 10 or more.

Distribution: Western North Atlantic from Trinidad, Jamaica, and the Gulf of Mexico to Long Island, New York. One record exists from the English Channel. They can be seen in deep waters around the Bahamas in spring.

Migration: No information is available.

Natural history notes: The estimated longevity is at least 17 years.

GINKGO-TOOTHED BEAKED WHALE

Japanese beaked whale

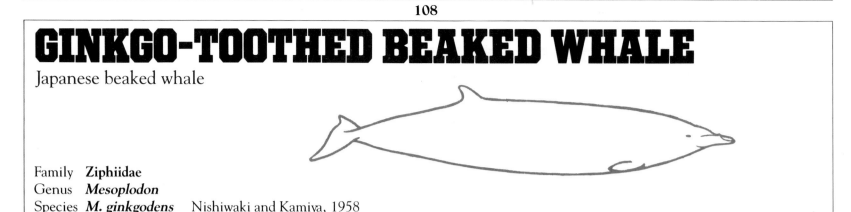

Family **Ziphiidae**
Genus *Mesoplodon*
Species ***M. ginkgodens***   Nishiwaki and Kamiya, 1958

These rare whales were named for their teeth, which resemble the leaves of the ginkgo tree. Until recently they were known from only three specimens, all caught incidentally in fishing lines in the Sea of Japan in 1963. Since then others have been found stranded in different parts of the Pacific and Indian Oceans, although many of these were immatures whose teeth had not erupted (they erupt only in the males), making positive identification extremely difficult.

Physical description: Body long and uniformly stocky, typical of beaked whales. The long beak protrudes smoothly from the melon, which is slightly indented at the blowhole. The lower jaw rises roundly along the sides where a flap of skin touches the upper jaw. Typical wishbone indentations are present on the throat.

Color: Midnight black; chest and abdominal regions lighter, including white scars from parasites, bacteria, and, possibly, fights with others of its species.

Fins and flukes: The small, pointed, falcate dorsal fin is located well to the rear of the midback region. Small, thin flippers are located relatively far forward. Well-developed, well-spread flukes have a slight median notch.

Length and weight: These whales reach a known length of 5.5 m (18 ft) and an estimated 1,450 kg (3,200 lb).

Teeth: A pair of flat, laterally compressed teeth is located behind the point at which the lower jaw bones meet. No teeth are found in the upper jaw. Teeth do not erupt in females.

Feeding: Squid and pelagic fish.

Breathing and diving: No information is available.

Mating and breeding: It has been suggested that 2.1 m (7 ft) calves are born in spring.

Herding: Specimens were stranded individually, suggesting that these animals swim alone.

Distribution: Recorded specimens are from Sri Lanka, Taiwan, Japan, and California.

Migration: No information is available.

GRAY'S BEAKED WHALE

scamperdown whale

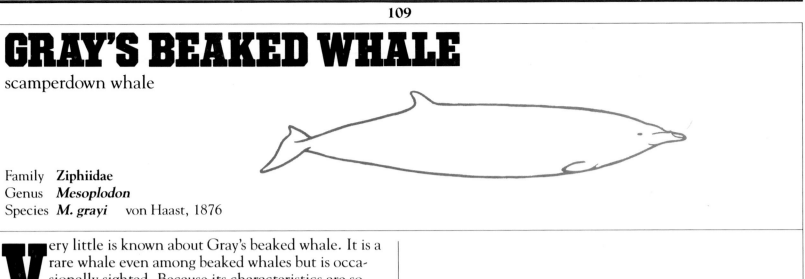

Family **Ziphiidae**
Genus **Mesoplodon**
Species **M. grayi**   von Haast, 1876

Very little is known about Gray's beaked whale. It is a rare whale even among beaked whales but is occasionally sighted. Because its characteristics are so clearly delineated, it is considered the "typical" beaked whale.

Physical description: The body is uniformly stocky and higher than it is wide. The rostrum is long, thin, and pointed. The upper jaw smoothly meets the melon, which dips to an indentation at the blowhole. The blowhole is wide and located slightly to the left of the forehead. Very well-defined wishbone indentations are found on the throat.

Color: Gray-green ranging to pale brown-green on ventral regions.

Fins and flukes: A comparatively large triangular dorsal fin has a slightly falcate curve at the tip, located two-thirds of the way back on the body. Very short, pointed flippers are wider than those of any other *Mesoplodon*. Well-developed flukes point backward at their tips, with no median notch.

Length and weight: Reaches 5.5 to 6 m (18 to 20 ft) and about 770 kg (1,700 lb).

Teeth: A pair of small triangular teeth is set well back from the tip of the lower jaw in males. Occasionally a row of small maxillary teeth is present in the upper jaw.

Feeding: Squid are known to be consumed.

Breathing and diving: No information is available.

Mating and breeding: It has been suggested that 2.1 m (7 ft) calves are born in spring.

Herding: In 1874 a group of 28 Gray's beaked whales beached themselves on Chatham Island off New Zealand, suggesting that the species does form herds. Otherwise unknown.

Distribution: South America, South Australia, New Zealand, Chatham Islands, and Argentina; one record from the Netherlands.

Migration: No information is available.

HUBBS' BEAKED WHALE

archbeak whale

Family **Ziphiidae**
Genus *Mesoplodon*
Species *M. carlhubbsi*   Moore, 1963

Illustrated by Larry A. Foster

Described in 1963 by J. C. Moore, this animal is known from fewer than a dozen strandings, the first discovered in 1944. Some researchers believe that Hubbs' beaked whale, Stejneger's beaked whale (page 112), and Andrews' beaked whale (page 113) are geographic variations of the same animal, for they are similar in many details. The paucity of specimens is in part to blame for the taxonomic controversy. Stejneger's and Andrew's beaked whales are little known and are described briefly on the following pages.

Physical description: Stocky body. The lower jaw extends slightly ahead of the upper jaw. The throat displays the typical wishbone indentation.

Color: All black except for the white tip of the rostrum and the white forehead. Small light spots cover the body.

Fins and flukes: The small falcate dorsal fin is located at the extreme rear of the midback region. Thin flippers appear disproportionately small compared with the body. Well-developed flukes are pointed at the tips, with no median notch.

Length and weight: Reach at least 5.2 m (17 ft).

Teeth: A pair of teeth, flattened and rounded at the tips, is located on the sides of the lower jaw in males. These teeth are about 9 cm (3.5 in) long, 16 to 16.5 cm (6.25 to 6.5 in) deep, and .65 cm (.25 in) broad, and have a straight leading edge that faces forward and frequently is found to be worn.

Feeding: Squid and mesopelagic fish.

Breathing and diving: No information is available.

Mating and breeding: Calving season is estimated to be in midsummer.

Herding: Groups of up to 10 are likely.

Distribution: Temperate waters of the North Pacific from Japan east to British Columbia and California.

Migration: No information is available.

This illustration of a Hubbs' beaked whale reveals the characteristic white areas on the tip of the rostrum and forehead, and the disproportionately small flippers.

STEJNEGER'S BEAKED WHALE

saber-toothed beaked whale

Family **Ziphiidae**
Genus ***Mesoplodon***
Species ***M. stejnegeri***   True, 1885

Physical description: The description is basically that of Hubbs' beaked whale (page 110).

Color: Same as Hubbs' beaked whale but without white coloring on head.

Length and weight: This whale reaches at least 5.3 m (17.3 ft) and 1,500 kg (3,300 lb).

Teeth: Both structure and position are the same as in Hubbs' beaked whale. The teeth are about 20 cm (8 in) long, 16 to 16.5 cm (6.25 to 6.5 in) deep, and 4 cm (1.5 in) broad.

Feeding: Known to feed on squid and salmon in Sea of Japan.

Breathing and diving: No information is available.

Mating and breeding: No information is available.

Herding: It is suggested that they swim in groups of 4 to 5.

Distribution: Subarctic waters of the North Pacific from the Bering Sea south to Japan and Oregon.

Migration: No information is available.

ANDREWS' BEAKED WHALE

Family **Ziphiidae**
Genus **Mesoplodon**
Species **M. bowdoini**   Andrews, 1908

Physical description: Basically that of Hubbs' beaked whale (page 110).

Color: Same as Hubb's beaked whale but without white coloring on head.

Length and weight: The Andrews' beaked whale reaches 4.6 m (15 ft) in length and 1,300 kg (2,900 lb). It is the smallest of the beaked whales.

Teeth: A pair of large, flattened teeth is set in partly raised sockets just behind the tip of the jaw. A small denticle on the tip of each tooth projects forward and outward. No teeth are found in the upper jaw.

Feeding: Squid.

Breathing and diving: No information is available.

Mating and breeding: No information is available.

Herding: No information is available.

Distribution: Known only from New Zealand, Tasmania, western Australia, Victoria, and the Kerguelen Islands.

Migration: No information is available.

SOWERBY'S BEAKED WHALE
North Sea beaked whale

Family **Ziphiidae**
Genus **Mesoplodon**
Species **M. bidens**   (Sowerby, 1804)

Sowerby's beaked whale is the most northerly of all beaked whales, and no other is likely to be found in its waters. It has the further distinction of being the first beaked whale ever discovered, in 1800, when one of the animals stranded at Moray Firth, Scotland.

Physical description: Body is long and thin for a *Mesoplodon*. The lower jaw protrudes ahead of the upper jaw from an elongated beak. The upper jaw smoothly meets the rising forehead, which drops slightly at the indentation of the blowhole. A pronounced bulge rises in front of the blowhole. The throat has typical wishbone indentations.

Color: Charcoal gray with occasional blue tint; white patches are evident on ventral regions of some animals; scratches, wounds, and light-colored scars are visible on most individuals, probably inflicted by others of the same species.

Fins and flukes: A well-defined, falcate dorsal fin is located far to the rear of the midback region. Small, short flippers are somewhat paddle shaped. Flukes are well developed, well spread, pointed backward at their tips, with no median notch.

Length and weight: Males are known to reach more than 5 m (16.5 ft); females just over 4.9 m (16 ft). The average weight is 1,270 kg (2,800 lb).

Teeth: A pair of teeth is found in the lower jaw midway between the tip and the gape. No teeth are present in the upper jaw. Teeth seldom erupt through the gums in females; those in adult males are barely visible.

Feeding: Squid and small fish.

Breathing and diving: No information is available.

Mating and Breeding: Breeding season lasts from February to April. A calf estimated at 2 m (6.5 ft) is born in late winter or spring after a 12-month gestation period. Lactation lasts 12 months, at which time the calf is 3 m (9.75 ft) in length.

Herding: Pairs have been reported off Iceland.

Distribution: Cool, temperate waters of the North Atlantic, from Newfoundland and Massachusetts east to southern Norway and the Bay of Biscay.

Migration: Individuals are found sometimes in the Newfoundland region in summer, presumably following prey species.

STRAP-TOOTHED WHALE

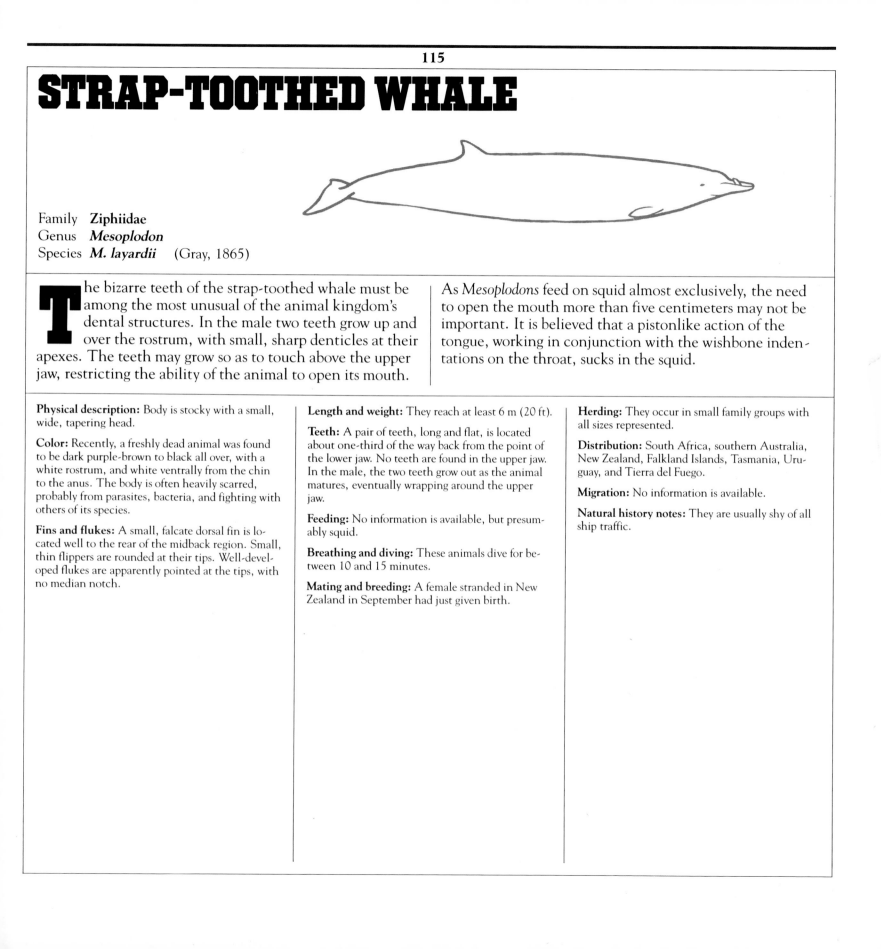

Family **Ziphiidae**
Genus **Mesoplodon**
Species **M. layardii**   (Gray, 1865)

The bizarre teeth of the strap-toothed whale must be among the most unusual of the animal kingdom's dental structures. In the male two teeth grow up and over the rostrum, with small, sharp denticles at their apexes. The teeth may grow so as to touch above the upper jaw, restricting the ability of the animal to open its mouth.

As *Mesoplodons* feed on squid almost exclusively, the need to open the mouth more than five centimeters may not be important. It is believed that a pistonlike action of the tongue, working in conjunction with the wishbone indentations on the throat, sucks in the squid.

Physical description: Body is stocky with a small, wide, tapering head.

Color: Recently, a freshly dead animal was found to be dark purple-brown to black all over, with a white rostrum, and white ventrally from the chin to the anus. The body is often heavily scarred, probably from parasites, bacteria, and fighting with others of its species.

Fins and flukes: A small, falcate dorsal fin is located well to the rear of the midback region. Small, thin flippers are rounded at their tips. Well-developed flukes are apparently pointed at the tips, with no median notch.

Length and weight: They reach at least 6 m (20 ft).

Teeth: A pair of teeth, long and flat, is located about one-third of the way back from the point of the lower jaw. No teeth are found in the upper jaw. In the male, the two teeth grow out as the animal matures, eventually wrapping around the upper jaw.

Feeding: No information is available, but presumably squid.

Breathing and diving: These animals dive for between 10 and 15 minutes.

Mating and breeding: A female stranded in New Zealand in September had just given birth.

Herding: They occur in small family groups with all sizes represented.

Distribution: South Africa, southern Australia, New Zealand, Falkland Islands, Tasmania, Uruguay, and Tierra del Fuego.

Migration: No information is available.

Natural history notes: They are usually shy of all ship traffic.

BLAINVILLE'S BEAKED WHALE

dense-beaked whale

Family **Ziphiidae**
Genus **Mesoplodon**
Species **M. densirostris** (de Blainville, 1817)

Another rare species of beaked whale, Blainville's beaked whale is known only from a few dozen strandings and a few sightings at sea. It is the only animal of its genus known to inhabit the tropical zone, although others may do so.

Physical description: Distinct beak with each corner of the mouth rising to a round contour, most prominent in adult males. Typical wishbone-shaped grooves are found on the throat.

Color: Black dorsal regions, somewhat lighter ventrally. The entire body may be blotched with lighter colors, and older animals tend to be scarred extensively.

Fins and flukes: A small dorsal fin is located to the rear of the midback region; it may be triangular or falcate. Small flippers are located behind and below the eyes in the lighter region of the lower flanks. Well-developed flukes are pointed at the tips, with a barely discernible median notch.

Length and weight: They reach at least 5.2 m (17 ft) and an estimated 2,400 kg (5,300 lb).

Teeth: Males have a 15 cm (6 in) triangular tooth on each side of mouth; females do not appear to have visible teeth.

Feeding: No information is available.

Breathing and diving: No information is available.

Mating and breeding: A calf was observed in the month of April.

Herding: These whales have been observed in groups of 3 to 6.

Distribution: Tropical and warm temperate waters of all oceans.

Migration: No information is available.

Barnacles encrust the teeth of this adult male Blainville's beaked whale.

Randall S. Wells

Chris Newbert

A Blainville's beaked whale reveals its characteristically prominent beak and massive lower jaw.

OCEANIC DOLPHINS
FAMILY: DELPHINIDAE

rough-toothed dolphin	Fraser's dolphin	northern right whale dolphin
Indo-Pacific hump-backed dolphin	white-beaked dolphin	southern right whale dolphin
Atlantic hump-backed dolphin	Atlantic white-sided dolphin	Risso's dolphin
Tucuxi dolphin	Pacific white-sided dolphin	melon-headed whale
bottlenose dolphin	dusky dolphin	pygmy killer whale
spinner dolphin	Peale's dolphin	false killer whale
short-snouted spinner dolphin	hourglass dolphin	long-finned pilot whale
spotted dolphin	Commerson's dolphin	short-finned pilot whale
Atlantic spotted dolphin	Chilean dolphin	killer whale
striped dolphin	Heaviside's dolphin	Irrawaddy dolphin
common dolphin	Hector's dolphin	

DEPENDING on what is considered to be a valid species, and also upon whether one lumps several diverse cetacean groups within the family, there are at least thirty and perhaps more than fifty species within the family Delphinidae, making it the largest family of cetaceans.

Cetologists have split or lumped these species throughout the history of taxonomy, and the situation is further confused because a three-foot dolphin and a 30-foot whale are both included in the family Delphinidae with almost every other toothy cetacean in between.

We have lumped all of the dolphinlike creatures with identical conical teeth in the family Delphinidae, but we recognize and emphasize that much of the information essential to the proper ordering of this family, or these families, is not available. As Frederick True, an early authority on the cetaceans, advised, " . . . cetologists must be content to wait patiently until the acquisition of new specimens makes a complete description possible." As a result of incidental take in fishing operations, direct harvests, and increased interest in cetaceans in general, many more specimens are available today than when Dr. True reviewed the Delphinidae in 1889, but many of the issues concerning relationships remain unresolved.

The questions exist in part because modern dolphins have been successful in occupying many diverse habitats and roles, and also because we humans like to classify all living things in an orderly way that suits our curatorial purposes. Unfortunately, the natural cycle of evolution is a continuous process that defies static definition. At almost every taxonomic line we draw there will be controversy, because we want our classification to be neat and tidy, like the books on the shelves of a rarely visited library. In any case, only we care; it appears to make no difference to the dolphins how we classify them.

All of the species included here have numerous conical teeth, with variations in number and arrangement among the species related to efficiency in catching their various prey species. All of these dolphins also exhibit compression and fusion of the neck vertebrae, which limits head mobility but contributes to the spindle-shaped body form adapted for high-speed swimming. All have developed sophisticated echolocation capabilities that are superior to their vision in perceiving their environment, and all have specialized anatomical features related to their acoustic ability. Most are gregarious and seem to have developed elaborate social structures, including seemingly sophisticated forms of acoustic communication. These sounds associated with communication have received a great deal of attention from a number of investigators, some of whom hope to establish a system of dolphin-human communication. However, as we have noted earlier, while dolphins are clearly highly intelligent animals, they live in a world very different from ours, and it is not clear that their communication takes a form that "says" something in our terms. Of course, they may be brighter than we imagine, and simply have nothing to say to us.

The diversity and adaptability of the dolphin group as a whole is well demonstrated by such species as *Tursiops truncatus* (the bottlenose dolphin) and *Orcinus orca* (the killer whale) both of which are popular animals at oceanaria throughout the world. Their ability to survive captivity and learn from and teach their trainers in such situations is legendary. Their behavior in captivity has contributed greatly to an increased public appreciation of all cetaceans. ➤

A pair of Atlantic spotted dolphins swims off Grand | **Bimini Island. More robust than their Pacific counterparts,** | **these dolphins resemble bottlenose dolphins with spots.**

Robert Pitman

ROUGH-TOOTHED DOLPHIN

Family **Delphinidae**
Genus *Steno*
Species *S. bredanensis*   (Lesson, 1828)

Named for the rough surface that forms near the crowns of their teeth, these animals are further distinguished by the smooth slope of their faces from beak to forehead; in the typical bottlenose dolphin the demarcation is far more prominent. The rough-toothed dolphin's compact, spindle-shaped body is clearly built for speed; some rough-toothed dolphins can attain speeds in excess of 24 kmph (15 mph). Infrequently, rough-toothed dolphins have been kept in captivity in both Japan and Hawaii, where their behavior suggested they possessed greater intelligence than do other marine mammals kept in captivity. One Hawaiian specimen, rewarded for developing new behavioral patterns, displayed an array of dolphin creativity including swimming at the surface upside-down with its tail raised out of the water.

Physical description: Unique among the beaked dolphins in its lack of a discernible demarcation line between the beak and forehead.

Color: Unusual mixture of gray, white, and pink multicolored blotches. Dark gray dorsally including the flippers and flukes. Beak and belly are white back to the anus.

Fins and flukes: A large, falcate dorsal fin is located on the midback region. Flippers are well developed and rounded at their tips. Flukes are small, rounded at the tips, with a well-defined median notch.

Length and weight: This dolphin reaches 2.3 to 2.7 m (7.5 to 9 ft) and 160 kg (350 lb).

Teeth: 20 to 27 fairly large, conical teeth with vertically wrinkled crowns are found in each side of the upper and lower jaws.

Feeding: Known to feed on small fish, pelagic octopus, and squid.

Breathing and diving: No reliable information.

Mating and breeding: Unknown.

Herding: Apparently 3 to 8 or more are normal, but herds of several hundred have been reported.

Distribution: Distributed throughout temperate seas of the Atlantic, Pacific, and Indian Oceans.

Natural history notes: A rough-toothed dolphin at Sea Life Park in Hawaii mated with a bottlenose dolphin which gave birth to a healthy calf with characteristics of both species. Rough-toothed dolphins are avid bow-wave riders.

Below, many scientists consider the rough-toothed dolphin to be the most intelligent of all the smaller dolphins. One animal, "Poko," was taught nearly two hundred new behavioral patterns at Sea Life Park in Hawaii.

Robert Pitman

W.J. Houck

Robert Pitman

Above, this playful rough-toothed dolphin displays a characteristic unique to this species, a well-defined beak with no demarcation between forehead and rostrum.

Left, extremely sociable animals, rough-toothed dolphins rarely pass up the chance to ride the bow-wave of a passing ship.

INDO-PACIFIC HUMP-BACKED DOLPHIN

Family **Delphinidae**
Genus *Sousa*
Species *S. chinensis* (Osbeck, 1765)

Taxonomic note: The problems involved in classification of cetaceans in general are amply illustrated with the Indo-Pacific hump-backed dolphin in that three separate taxonomic names—*Sousa lentiginosa, Sousa plumbea,* and *Sousa borneensis*—have been proposed for animals that are generally recognized as variations of *Sousa chinensis.*

Like many other cetaceans, the Indo-Pacific hump-backed dolphin is often seen but rarely studied in its native habitat. It lives in shallow waters near coasts and penetrates into estuaries. There have been reports that this species traverses mud banks. If so, it would be only the third cetacean species known to remove itself from the water, the other two being the Amazon River dolphin (page 198) and bottlenose dolphin (page 125). The claim is at least plausible since the animal's ability to negotiate changing tidal depths is well known.

Physical description: This animal superficially resembles the bottlenose dolphin but has a thinner beak and the shape of the dorsal fin varies with geographical distribution.

Color: These dolphins are ivory colored with a pink ventral region. The fins and flukes are a mixture of brown and pink.

Fins and flukes: The triangular dorsal fin is rounded at the tip. The hump-and-fin dorsal fin configuration (described for the Atlantic hump-backed dolphin, page 123) appears only on animals found west of Indonesia: animals found east of Indonesia have a simple dorsal fin. The flippers are small, paddle shaped, and rounded at the tips, while the flukes are well-developed, pointed at the tips, with a slight median notch.

Length and weight: They reach 3 m (9.75 ft) in length and an estimated 150 kg (330 lb).

Teeth: They possess 32 to 37 small, conical teeth in each side of the upper jaw; 32 to 34 in each side of the lower jaw.

Feeding: Their habits are little known. They appear to feed mostly on fish.

Breathing and diving: Indo-Pacific hump-backed dolphins are slow swimmers, breathing every minute or so after rising to the surface at a steep angle, often exposing the head and rostrum. When diving they arch the back dramatically.

Mating and breeding: Newborns are 90 cm (35.5 in) and 25 kg (55 lb). Calves are born year-round, with a peak in summer months.

Herding: They are found individually or in herds of up to 20. Six is usual.

Distribution: Subpopulations are found in the coastal waters of the Indian and western Pacific oceans (*Sousa plumbea*), from Port Elizabeth, South Africa, north to the Red Sea (*Sousa lentiginosa*), and east to southern China, including the lower reaches of the Yangtze, Foochow, and Canton rivers; Borneo, and northeastern and eastern Australia (*Sousa borneensis*).

Migration: No information is available.

Natural history notes: Often they are extremely active when on the surface, swimming on their sides, and young animals are known to leap from the water. They are found often with bottlenose dolphins (page 125) and finless porpoises (page 212).

The juvenile Indo-Pacific hump-backed dolphin's small flippers, long and thin beak, and small forehead distinguish it from the bottlenose dolphin.

Grant Abel

ATLANTIC HUMP-BACKED DOLPHIN

Cameroon dolphin

Family **Delphinidae**
Genus *Sousa*
Species ***S. teuszii*** (Kukenthal, 1892)

Not all cetaceans roam the open oceans; some, such as the Atlantic hump-backed dolphin, prefer to inhabit a limited stretch of water. Although this species is known to live along the west coast of Africa from Senegal to Cameroon, little information has been gathered and few photographs taken. Until recently, this dolphin was known from a single damaged specimen found by a Mr. Teuz in 1892. Several more have been discovered near Dakar in recent years and researchers are assembling information on their life history. Although the animal is known as a hump-backed dolphin, the nature of its hump—whether related to age, sex, or another factor—is unclear.

Recent aerial observations have revealed that these dolphins use waves or strong swells to gain momentum in diving for food; dives may last for up to three minutes. Observations of older and larger adult animals show them to be heavily scarred on the flanks and dorsal regions. Young adult animals are unscarred and uniformly gray, giving them the nickname "graybacks." Animals of all ages have been observed leaping clear of the water, sometimes performing complete reverse somersaults. Rapid swimming and chasing were also evident.

Physical description: Except for the narrower body and smaller flippers, they resemble bottlenose dolphins (page 125). The beak is well-defined with a demarcation line between the beak and a small melon. The blowhole projects up from the forehead, forming a small hump.

Color: Adults exhibit whitening of the dorsal fin and adjacent areas, extending occasionally from the tip of the rostrum to the flukes—this appears to be a phenomenon of increased age. The average animal is slate gray on the sides, paler gray ventrally.

Fins and flukes: The dorsal fin rises gradually into a falcate fin. From information available, it appears the flippers are small and rounded at their edges. Flukes are thin, well developed, and pointed at the tips, with a slight median notch.

Length and weight: Up to 2.8 m (9.25 ft) and 290 kg (630 lb).

Teeth: 26 to 31 per side are found in both upper and lower jaws, separated by spaces.

Feeding: Small fish, caught as the herd disperses in all directions.

Breathing and diving: The dive lasts for at least 3 minutes.

Mating and breeding: There appears to be no birthing season, although a peak of births is apparent in summer months.

Herding: Atlantic hump-backed dolphins often are found individually or in pairs; groups of up to 20 are not uncommon.

Distribution: They are most common in waters near Senegal, especially Dakar, ranging to the Cameroons of the west coast of Africa. They were discovered in the harbor of Douala, Cameroon. Apparently they are restricted to coastal areas and river estuaries.

Migration: Apparently does not migrate.

Natural history notes: These animals have been seen swimming with bottlenose dolphins.

G.S. Saayman

This rare aerial photograph of a pod of Atlantic hump-backed dolphins was taken off the coast of South Africa. The "knuckled" dorsal fin indicates adulthood.

TUCUXI DOLPHIN

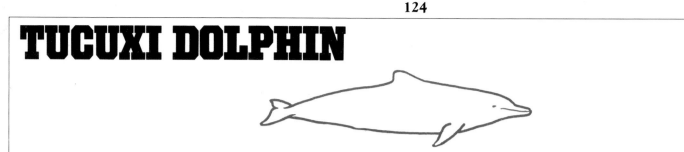

Family **Delphinidae**
Genus *Sotalia*
Species ***S. fluviatilis*** (Gervais, 1853)

Taxonomic note: Some variations have been labeled as subspecies: Guiana dolphin, *Sotalia guianensis*; Brazilian dolphin, *Sotalia brasiliensis*; buffeo blanco (dolphin), *Sotalia pallida*. These appear to be merely color variations of the same animal. Another seldom used name for the tucuxi dolphin is *Sotalia tucuxi*.

This, the smallest of all cetaceans, is a fluvial animal, inhabiting coastal regions near the mouths of rivers and advancing into such rivers as the Amazon and Orinoco. It does not possess the long, narrow beak and paddle-shaped flippers ordinarily associated with river dolphins, but looks more like the much larger bottlenose dolphin (page 125). The animal's distribution appears to have something to do with its color, since the clear-water fluvial populations are somewhat darker than the cloudy-water Amazonian populations.

Physical description: As noted, the body shape is similar to that of the bottlenose dolphin. The animal possesses a thick, well-developed beak with pronounced demarcation from a sloping melon.

Color: The body is brown-gray overall, lightening to a cream color in the ventral region. The dark dorsal color extends down in a blade shape from the upper back on each side, disappearing near the anus. All fins are the color of the dorsal region.

Fins and flukes: The well-developed dorsal fin is falcate, pointed at the tip, and located on the mid-back region. The flippers are broad and pointed, while the flukes are thin, broad, rounded at the tips, and possess a well-defined median notch.

Length and weight: These animals reach a length of 1.9 m (6.25 ft) and a weight of between 32 and 36 kg (70 and 80 lb).

Teeth: There are 26 to 35 teeth in each side of the upper and lower jaws.

Feeding: They take armored catfish and freshwater crustaceans.

Breathing and diving: Those animals found in rivers are known to raise much of the head out of the water when breathing; short leaps from the water are not uncommon. Time underwater between blows averages about 33 seconds.

Mating and breeding: Calves, 68 to 79 cm (27 to 31 in), black above and white below, have been observed between February and March. Gestation is believed to be 10 months.

Herding: They are solitary or travel in groups of 6 to 7.

Distribution: A very small population is found 1,900 km (1,200 mi) and farther up the Amazon River, where these dolphins swim with Amazon River dolphins (page 198). They are found along the coast of Surinam and other coastal regions of South America.

Migration: No significant or predictable migration has been observed.

Natural history notes: These animals are comfortable in freshwater, brackish, and saltwater environments. The movements of animals found in rivers seem dependent on river conditions—drought and flooding.

The smallest of all dolphins, the tucuxi resembles the bottlenose dolphin except for the pointed and triangular dorsal fin and other more subtle differences.

Courtesy Marineland of Florida

BOTTLENOSE DOLPHIN

Family **Delphinidae**
Genus **Tursiops**
Species **T. truncatus** (Montagu, 1821)

Taxonomic note: A variety of taxonomic labels exists for bottlenose dolphins found in different regions of the world. The name *Tursiops truncatus* encompasses all of them in a general sense. However, many researchers believe that the size, physical appearance, color, and slight physical variations are dramatic enough to warrant at least two more distinct species, although perhaps subspecies classification would be more in line with the differences. These species are the North Pacific bottlenose dolphin, *Tursiops gilli;* Southern Hemisphere bottlenose dolphin, *Tursiops aduncus.* References to other populations of bottlenose dolphins that are occasionally used can generally be considered to be within *Tursiops truncatus.*

Perhaps the best known of all cetaceans, the bottlenose dolphin is the species most commonly kept in oceanaria and research facilities. Its brain is larger than a human's, and in captivity it is a curious, alert, cooperative animal, friendly toward humans and other dolphins alike. While they are very wary and difficult to capture, they adapt readily once caught and have invented complex behavioral patterns of their own. In fact, the animal does so well in captivity that there is now a fifth generation of captive bottlenose dolphins. In the wild they are accustomed to shallow water and have been seen many times riding the surf.

Physical description: Theirs is generally considered to be the typical Delphinidae body form. The body is long and somewhat stocky. The melon is well-defined where the beak meets the forehead. The lower jaw extends beyond the upper jaw, curving slightly upward at its tip.

Color: Dark gray dorsally to lighter gray on flanks and white or near pink on ventral region.

Fins and flukes: A prominent falcate dorsal fin is located at the midback region. Medium-sized flippers are well spread and somewhat rounded at their tips, with the leading edges curved toward the body. Flukes are well spread, thin, and somewhat rounded at the tips, with a well-defined median notch.

Length and weight: This dolphin reaches 4 m (13 ft) and 650 kg (1,450 lb). Some authorities propose a smaller form which reaches 3 m (9.75 ft).

Teeth: There are 18 to 26 small, sharp, conical teeth in each of the upper and lower jaws.

Feeding: Small fish, eels, catfish, mullet, and squid.

Breathing and diving: When swimming, bottlenose dolphins rise to the surface to breathe every 15 to 20 seconds, although they can remain underwater for at least several minutes while riding bowwaves.

Mating and breeding: After a one-year gestation period, 90 to 130 cm (35 to 50 in) calves are born between February and May—and possibly between September and November—in Florida waters, and during midsummer in European waters. Lactation lasts 12 to 18 months. Sexual maturity is reached at 10 to 12 years in males, 5 to 12 years in females. Females are thought to be capable of 8 births over a lifetime, at 2- to 3-year intervals.

Herding: Usually several hundred broken into pods of about one dozen. Smaller herds of up to 40 are often observed off Florida.

Distribution: Worldwide in temperate and tropical waters.

Migration: No information is available.

Natural history notes: "Babysitting" behavior has been observed, in which another adult attends the infant of a female while she is out feeding. The lifespan is believed to be 35 years or more.

After nursing for about a year, this juvenile bottlenose dolphin will be weaned and ready for a diet of solid food.

Marineland of Florida

Gerard Wellington

Above, while bottlenose dolphin distribution is worldwide, those of the Pacific Ocean, such as these animals in the Galapagos Islands, often appear more scarred and darker in coloration than those in other locations.

Right, the bottlenose dolphin is perhaps the most familiar of all cetaceans, well known for its popularity in oceanaria, its cosmopolitan distribution and appearance on the *Flipper* television show.

Robert Pitman

SPINNER DOLPHINS

Family **Delphinidae**
Genus ***Stenella***
Species ***S. longirostris*** (Gray, 1828)

Taxonomic note: There are a wide variety of spinner dolphins, all but one of which are currently classified as *Stenella longirostris*. Although these varieties are not recognized as separate species, they have been given popular common names by researchers working closely with the given populations. Below are the indicated common names with variant descriptions, based on contemporary and ongoing research.

One of the more delicate looking *Stenellas*, the spinner dolphin has a long, graceful beak and a petite overall appearance. The animal can be identified at sea by its practice of leaping and spinning as it swims. Whether this behavior is as playful and frivolous as it appears, or has a serious biological purpose, remains to be determined.

Spinner dolphins of the eastern tropical Pacific Ocean associate with schools of yellowfin tuna, a relationship which has led to their being killed by the hundreds of thousands during purse-seine tuna-fishing operations of the past 20 years.

As discussed in the taxonomic note, spinners are bunched into one distinct species, *Stenella longirostris*, although there are dramatic variations among geographic populations.

Whereas sexual dimorphism does not occur in many species of the cetaceans, certain eastern tropical Pacific Ocean spinner herds do have obvious physical distinctions between females and males. Males possess a bump, or protuberance, on the ventral peduncle, and a forward cant to the dorsal fin that to the casual observer may make it appear as though the fin were placed on backwards. Although there are theories concerning the presence of the protuberances and dorsal-fin cant, none has yet been proven. One guess seems to be that it allows females of one population to find males of the same population in conditions when herds are mixed.

Spinners may dive as deep at 61 m (200 ft) to feed. Calves are born at an estimated 80 cm (32 in) in length, and little else is known of their breeding habits. Almost nothing is known of their migratory habits.

Costa Rican spinner dolphin, also called long-snouted dolphin, has a long, slender body, with an elongated and delicate rostrum. They are dark gray dorsally, with a lighter color on the ventral region. The dorsal fin is tall, triangular, and canted toward the front in old males. The flippers are long, thin, and pointed at the tips. Costa Rican spinner dolphins are from 1.7 to 2.1 m (5.6 to 7 ft) long and weigh an estimated 68 kg (150 lb). There are an estimated 100 small, conical teeth in the upper and lower jaws. The known diet includes small fish and copepods. These dolphins herd in numbers of 1,000 or more and are found near the coast of Nicaragua, Costa Rica, and Panama.

Eastern spinner dolphin, also known as long-snouted dolphin, has a short, slender body with a short, heavy rostrum. This dolphin is similar in color to the Costa Rican spinner dolphin although it has the darkest dorsal region of all the spinners. Flippers and fins are similar to those of the Costa

Rican spinner. The ventral keel past the anal region displays a protuberance comprised of connective tissue which corresponds in size to the degree of forward cant of the dorsal fin. The length varies from 1.65 to 1.8 m (5.5 to 6 ft); weight averages 61 kg (135 lb). The eastern spinner has the same basic tooth count as the Costa Rican spinner. Gestation is believed to be 10.6 months. These dolphins are found in herds of 1,000 or more, often mixed with Pacific spotted dolphins (page 135). They are found along the coast of Mexico, extending out 1,900 km (1,200 mi).

Whitebelly spinner dolphin, also called long-snouted dolphin, has a short stocky body, dark, down to the eye level, on the dorsal side. The ventral region is white. The dorsal fin may be triangular or falcate; a slight protuberance is present along the ventral keel. Small, thin flippers are pointed at the tips. The average whitebelly length

is 1.75 m (5.75 ft); average weight, 61 kg (135 lb). The diet consists of small fish and copepods. The gestation of this dolphin is believed to be 10.6 months. They herd in numbers of 1,000 or more, and are often found with Pacific spotted dolphins (page 135). Whitebelly spinners are found in offshore Pacific waters of Mexico, Central America, and the Pacific side of northern South America, extending out nearly 322 km (200 mi), and overlapping the range of the eastern spinner dolphin.

Tropical Atlantic and Indian Ocean spinner dolphins may be called long-snouted dolphins. The two geographic herds are similar if not identical, and the length of the beak may vary with individual animals of herds of different regions. These animals are dark gray dorsally, lighter on the flanks and white on the ventral region. The tip of the rostrum and the lips are black. Adults may be very dark in color with white speckles. The dorsal fin is

William High. NMFS

smaller than that of the eastern tropical Pacific animals and is falcate. The flippers are long and pointed. These dolphins reach a length of 1.8 to 2.1 m (6 to 7 ft), and weight an estimated 82 kg (180 lb). There are from 92 to 130 small, conical teeth in each of the upper and lower jaws. The known diet includes small fish and copepods. These animals herd in numbers of several hundred or more, and are distributed throughout the tropical Atlantic, the Gulf of Mexico, and most of the Indian Ocean.

Hawaiian spinner dolphin, previously referred to taxonomically as *Stenella roseiventris,* is a streamlined animal with a long, thin rostrum. It has a distinctive three-toned color pattern. The area from the rostrum to just past the dorsal fin is dark gray, the flanks are a lighter gray, and the ventral region

is white. The dorsal fin is falcate but smaller than those of other Pacific spinners. Flippers are long, thin, and pointed at the tips. These dolphins reach a length of up to 2.1 m (7 ft) and a weight of 91 kg (200 lb). There are 100 small, conical teeth in both upper and lower jaws. The diet includes small fish. The Hawaiian spinners herd in numbers of about 200 usually and often are found with humpback whales when the larger animals migrate to Hawaiian waters during the winter (page 56). These spinners are found readily in Hawaiian waters, but have been reported as far east as San Diego.

The relationship between spinner dolphins and yellowfin tuna has led to the deaths of hundreds of thousands of dolphins when they have become entangled and drowned in mile-long tuna nets like this one.

A spinner dolphin off Hawaii breaches and twists into a spin, a maneuver that gives the species its name.

Randall S. Wells

Left, an eastern Pacific spinner dolphin exhibits a dark gray color pattern which may be characteristic of this animal's particular herd.

Below, a pair of spinner dolphins, perhaps a mating couple, swims in the clear waters of the eastern tropical Pacific.

Robert Pitman

Robert Pitman

SHORT-SNOUTED SPINNER DOLPHIN

Clymene dolphin

Family **Delphinidae**
Genus **Stenella**
Species **S. clymene** (Gray, 1850)

Taxonomic note: Until 1981, when William F. Perrin (senior author) authored *Stenella clymene, A Rediscovered Tropical Dolphin of the Atlantic*, the short-snouted spinner dolphin was considered a variation of *Stenella longirostris*.

The short-snouted spinner dolphin is a little-known animal of the Atlantic Ocean. Although it very much resembles the spinner dolphin *Stenella longirostris* (their range even overlaps in certain areas), it is doubtless a distinct species based on extensive skull and skeletal comparisons.

C.W. Oliver, NMFS

Left, this picture of a pair of short-snouted dolphins swimming off the northwest coast of Africa is the only photograph of this species ever taken in the wild.

Physical description: This animal looks much the same as *Stenella longirostris* (page 128) but the flippers and dorsal fin are about ten percent smaller. As the name implies, the rostrum is shorter, but also thicker than other spinners.

Color: These animals possess a distinct three toned color pattern. The dorsal region is dark from the melon to the mid-peduncle region, dropping down convexly along both sides. A grey region extends from eyes along the flanks encompassing the peduncle region to the area of the anus. The white coloration extends from the lower jaw back to the anus. The white field is flecked with very small irregular dots, most numerous where the white and grey regions meet. The color of the rostrum varies from all dark above, white on the sides with black trim along the upper and lower lips, to more uniformly dark overall, although the former seems most common. The flippers can be either all black (both sides) or dark underneath with white above trimmed along the leading margin with black. The eyes have a dark circle with a thin line extending to the demarcation of the rostrum.

Fins and flukes: The dorsal fin is well-defined, falcate, nearly pointed and located on the midback region. The flippers are a bit smaller than other spinners and pointed at the tips. The well spread flukes are thin and pointed at the tips with a well-defined median notch.

Length and weight: They reach a known length of 2 m (7 ft) and an estimated weight of 90 kg (200 lb).

Teeth: There are 38 to 49 sharply pointed teeth in each row of the upper and lower jaws.

Illustrated by Larry A. Foster

Feeding: They are known to feed on small fish and squid, and are thought to be mid-water or nocturnal feeders.

Mating and breeding: Almost nothing is known. It has been suggested that newborn are about 77 cm (30.3 in).

Herding: They are thought to form small herds.

Distribution: They are known from the tropical and subtropical Atlantic. Sightings have occured in the southeastern United States, Gulf of Mexico, Caribbean Sea, northwest coast of Africa, and the mid-Atlantic Ocean.

Migration: No information is available.

Natural history notes: These animals have been observed only in deep water. Spinning has been observed but was less dramatic and less complex than other spinners. In the Gulf of Guinea and off West Africa, they have been observed riding bow-waves.

Above, **a little-known animal, the short-snouted spinner dolphin illustrated here is found in the tropical and subtropical Atlantic Ocean.**

ATLANTIC SPOTTED DOLPHIN

Family **Delphinidae**
Genus *Stenella*
Species *S. plagiodon*   (Cope, 1866)

Taxonomic note: Currently all Atlantic spotted dolphins are considered to be *Stenella plagiodon*. However, William F. Perrin, a United States government biologist, is revising this philosophy through a soon-to-be-published paper that explains the need to distinguish *Stenella dubia*, *S. attenuata*, and *S. frontalis* (into which *S. plagiodon* will be absorbed) as separate species.

A variety of morphological differences, some slight and some dramatic, separate the different populations of *Stenella*. All *Stenella* are found in temperate and tropical waters throughout the world. The Atlantic spotted dolphin is distinguished from spinner and other spotted dolphins by its robust body, thick beak, and other characteristics more representative of bottlenose dolphins (page 125). They are, however, the most spotted of all dolphins at maturity.

Atlantic spotted dolphins are extremely friendly and inquisitive animals, traveling long distances to ride the bowwaves of passing vessels, and will swim within touching range of divers and swimmers.

Physical description: Closely resembles the bottlenose dolphin; the beak of the species is nearly identical both in shape and extension. The body is stocky with a disproportionately narrow peduncle region.

Color: Generally blue overall. The dorsal region is much darker than the ventral, extending down from midflanks to encompass the peduncle. The dark dorsal area is spotted extensively with lighter blue spots. Young are born a light color (resembling bottlenose dolphins) and develop the spotted coloration as they mature.

Fins and flukes: A falcate dorsal fin, very tall, is well developed and located on the midback region. Flippers are curved on their leading margins and pointed at the tips. Thin flukes are well spread and pointed at the tips.

Length and weight: Length is 2.3 m (7.5 ft), weight is estimated at 127 kg (280 lb).

Teeth: 34 to 37 small, conical teeth are found in each side of upper and lower jaws.

Feeding: Squid; probably also herring, anchovies, other small fish, and eels.

Breathing and diving: No information is available.

Mating and breeding: Calves, approximately 91 cm (3 ft) are believed to be born in June after a gestation period of perhaps 11 months.

Herding: Commonly 50 or fewer, the herds may reach several hundred.

Distribution: Atlantic coast of the United States, Gulf of Mexico, Bahamas; they also may inhabit the coast of South America and Europe. They are less abundant than other species of spotted dolphins.

Migration: The Gulf of Mexico population moves inshore during late spring, approaching close to shore then and during summer.

More robust than its Pacific counterpart, the Atlantic spotted dolphin closely resembles the bottlenose dolphin except for the dramatic spotting all over the body.

Courtesy Marineland of Florida

SPOTTED DOLPHIN

Family **Delphinidae**
Genus *Stenella*
Species *S. attenuata* (Gray, 1846)

Taxonomic note: There are many varieties of spotted dolphins found all around the world. Until more information is gathered on all of these herds, *Stenella attenuata* is commonly used to describe taxonomically all but the Atlantic spotted dolphins (p. 134). However, Indian Ocean and certain Pacific Ocean populations are occasionally referred to as *Stenella attenuata graffmani,* a subspecies.

Spotted dolphins are gregarious animals, as are the *Stenellas* generally, and are often seen in the company of other dolphin species. Like their relatives, the spinner dolphins (page 128) of the same region, eastern tropical Pacific herds associate closely with yellowfin tuna schools, an enigmatic relationship which has led incidentally to the killing of hundreds of thousands of these dolphins during commercial purse-seine tuna-fishing operations. Also like the spinners, the spotted dolphins occur in many seas, with slight physical differences among herds. This has led to suggestions for a further subdivision of species, subspecies, and races, but as yet too little is known of these animals to warrant such classification.

Unlike the spinner dolphins, which may dive as deep as 61 m (200 ft) for food, the spotted dolphins appear to be surface feeders.

Physical description: The body is long and thin with very well-developed delphinid characteristics. They very much resemble Atlantic spotted dolphins (page 134) in body form.

Color: There are slight variations among herds. The basic description is steel gray dorsally from the beak and just above the eyes to and including the flukes, and from the beak to and encompassing the eyes. The flanks and ventral areas are gray. The flippers are steel gray with an extended stripe from the leading margin to the rostrum. Normally, at least a portion of the tip of the rostrum is white, and in many cases the upper and lower lips are completely white. The dark parts of the body are covered with dense gray spots, and gray portions of the body are covered with lighter spots. In offshore populations, calves are purple-gray dorsally, white ventrally, with no spots. Juveniles become dark dorsally, light ventrally. Ventral spots appear with maturity, covering much of the body and often overlapping, showing a mottled coloration with light gray dorsal spots.

Fins and flukes: The dorsal fin is falcate and can be either slightly rounded or pointed. The flippers are small and for the most part pointed, and very well-defined. The flukes are small, pointed at the tips, with a small median notch.

Length and weight: Spotted dolphins reach about 2.1 m (7 ft) and an estimated weight of 127 kg (280 lb).

Teeth: They have between 41 and 45 small, conical teeth in each side of the upper and lower jaws.

Feeding: Little is known of their feeding habits. Their diet includes squid and surface-dwelling fish such as flying fish.

Breathing and diving: Spotted dolphins exhibit a "porpoising" behavior (long, shallow leaps clear of the water) as they swim.

Mating and breeding: Calves are born at about 80 cm (32 in) after a gestation period of about 11 months. Lactation lasts 11 months. Sexual maturity in males is reached at between 6 and 8 years at 2 m (6.75 ft); in females at 1.9 m (6.5 ft). Females are believed to give birth every two years, but this may be more often than might be the case in normal circumstances because of the stress placed on the populations by tuna fishing and consequent dolphin mortality.

Herding: Herds of up to 3,000 to 4,000 have been observed but the common herd is composed of a hundred or less.

Distribution: These animals are found throughout the tropical regions of the Pacific Ocean. They are known to occur in the South China Sea and the waters around Japan, and as far south as Australia and New Zealand.

William High, NMFS

Eastern tropical Pacific spotted dolphins mill around on the surface, trapped in a tuna net. Some herds of spotted dolphins have been caught so many times that they often wait patiently for release.

Migration: These animals appear to have complex migratory habits but we know very little about them.

Natural history notes: Although not wary of boats they seldom ride bow-waves.

Above, a spotted dolphin leaps horizontally clear of the water, exhibiting "porpoising" behavior.

Right, an eastern tropical Pacific spotted dolphin leaps next to a research vessel. Herds often exhibit subtle color variations that distinguish them from other herds in the same vicinity.

Robert Pitman

Robert Pitman

STRIPED DOLPHIN

streaker
blue-and-white
Euphrosyne dolphin

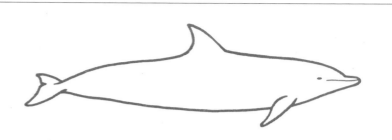

Family **Delphinidae**
Genus **Stenella**
Species **S. coeruleoalba**   (Meyen, 1833)

Taxonomic note: Herds with variant color patterns have in the past been referred to as *Stenella styx* or *Stenella euphrosyne*, although these names are rarely if ever used today and are not valid.

The striped dolphins are the largest and most robust of the five recognized *Stenella* species. While they are relatively numerous, they are not often known to ride bow-waves and will usually not approach ships, thus affording comparatively little opportunity for close-range study or observation. The blue blade-shape color pattern on the flanks and the thin dark stripe running from each eye along the lower flanks to the genital region add to the animals' distinctive appearance. In the eastern tropical Pacific Ocean, these animals have been known to associate with yellowfin tuna, although this relationship is extremely limited compared to spinner, spotted, and common dolphins of the same region.

Physical description: Robust animals as *Stenellas* go, with well-defined *Stenella* characteristics.

Color: The dorsal region is blue-black from the tip of the beak to midway between the tail and dorsal fin. Blue-black color continues from just behind the dorsal fin halfway to the eyes, narrowing to a blade-shaped stripe. Thin black stripes run from each eye converging near the anus. A second stripe begins at each eye and terminates above and just past the flippers. A third dark stripe runs from just under each eye terminating at the leading edge of the flippers. White flippers blend, where they join the body, with its dark areas.

Fins and flukes: A tall dorsal fin is falcate and situated on the midback region. Flippers are small and curved at their leading edges, pointed at the tips. Flukes are small, thin, and pointed at the tips, with a slight median notch.

Length and weight: This dolphin reaches about 2.7 m (9 ft) and 115 kg (250 lb).

Teeth: 45 to 50 small, conical teeth are found on each side of the upper jaw and 43 to 49 on each side of the lower jaw.

Feeding: Small fish, shrimp, squid, and other organisms.

Breathing and diving: No information is available.

Mating and breeding: Calves just over a meter (40 in) are born after a gestation period of approximately 12 months and weaned after 8 months. Sexual maturity is attained at 9 years. Striped dolphins are thought to have two distinct breeding seasons—spring and autumn. Females bear young every 2.5 or 3 years.

Herding: Groups may be from 10 to 40, apparently separated by age and sex.

Distribution: Worldwide in tropical and temperate waters.

Migration: No information is available.

Natural history notes: These animals are thought to live to at least 50 years.

Robert Pitman

Robert Pitman

Left, this group of striped dolphins is only a small part of a herd that may number over 2,000 individuals. Within the herd, some scientists believe, individuals group according to sex and age.

Above, striped dolphins reveal their complex and appealing color patterns. Scientists do not know what, if any, adaptive value the patterns have.

COMMON DOLPHIN
saddleback dolphin

Family **Delphinidae**
Genus *Delphinus*
Species ***D. delphis*** Linnaeus, 1758

Taxonomic note: Other names sometimes are used for variants of the common dolphin: Arabian Sea and Gulf of Aden common dolphin, *Delphinus tropicalis*; Cape of Good Hope to Gulf of Aden common dolphin, with limited distribution in the Atlantic and Japanese waters, *Delphinus capensis*; Black Sea common dolphin, *Delphinus delphis ponticius*.

Although they have been observed near shore, common dolphins more often congregate farther out to sea, sometimes in huge herds of 2,000 individuals or more. The animals will change course for the opportunity to ride the bow-wave of a passing ship.

As with certain species of *Stenella*, the eastern tropical Pacific common dolphin herds associate with yellowfin tuna. However, their ability to escape tuna nets, learned from experience, has earned them the name "untouchables" among tuna fishermen. Attempts to maintain common dolphins in marine parks or research facilities have often resulted in death from shock and apparent depression.

Until regional variants of the common dolphin are recognized as distinct species, subspecies, or races, all common dolphins will continue to be considered as a single species, *Delphinus delphis* (see taxonomic note).

Physical description: The body is long and slender with very well-defined features. The length of the beak and the color pattern are perhaps the best keys to identification among regional variants.

Color: The common dolphin's basic pattern is black dorsally from the beak to the center of the peduncle, extending downward under the dorsal fin in the shape of an upside-down triangle. The flanks are gray from the eye to the tail. The white color of the ventral region extends upwards at the sides in a triangle, the tip of which meets the darker dorsal triangle to form an hourglass or crisscross configuration. The rostrum is usually black with a white tip. The dark chin color extends broadly to the leading margin of the flippers where it blends with the dark flipper color. The demarcation of the beak and forehead is defined by a thin dark line extending out to meet the dark eye patch.

Fins and flukes: The prominent falcate dorsal fin is rounded at the top and located on the midback region. The dark flippers are long, thin, and slightly rounded or pointed, depending on regional variation. The flukes are thin, pointed at the tips, with a slight median notch.

Length and weight: These animals reach a length of 2.1 to 2.4 m (7 to 8 ft), and weigh between 91 and 136 kg (200 and 300 lb). Mature males are normally 10 to 20 cm (4 to 8 in) longer than females.

Teeth: An average of 40 to 50 small, pointed teeth are located in each side of the upper and lower jaws.

Feeding: Common dolphins feed on schools of migrating fish such as anchovies, herring, and sardines; also squid.

Breathing and diving: These animals can dive as deep as 280 m (900 ft) and remain down as long as eight minutes. There appears to be a daily cycle of activity during which small feeding groups scatter in the late afternoon to feed on the rising organisms in the deep scattering layer (DSL). When the DSL returns to deeper waters, the groups come together again for rest or social interaction.

Mating and breeding: Calves of 76 to 86 cm (30 to 34 in) are born every 1.3 years in spring and fall after a gestation period of between 10 and 11 months. Calves are weaned at between 1 and 3 years. Sexual maturity is reached when the animal is about 3 to 4 years old, 1.67 to 1.8 m (5.5 to 6 ft).

Herding: Herds of up to 3,000 are not uncommon.

Distribution: They are found in the North and South Pacific Ocean, the Indian Ocean, and are widely distributed in warmer temperate and tropical waters of all oceans including the Black Sea.

Migration: Most populations seem to follow the movements of food fish.

Robert Pitman

Above, a robust body and well-defined rostrum characterize the common dolphin. Abnormal coloration among individuals in a herd is not unusual; this animal lacks the crisscross patterning usually found on the flanks of common dolphins.

Right, the common dolphin is one of the few dolphin species to carry markings of three colors—white, black, and cream. Note the characteristic crisscross pattern on the flanks of this swift and energetic animal.

FRASER'S DOLPHIN

Sarawak dolphin

Family **Delphinidae**
Genus *Lagenodelphis*
Species **L. hosei**   Fraser, 1956

This species was originally described on the basis of a single skeleton obtained by a Mr. E. Hose from a western Borneo beach in 1895. It was not described from life until 1971, when several of the animals were caught in tuna nets in the eastern tropical Pacific Ocean. Also in 1971, another group of Fraser's dolphins was captured off the Philippines and transported to an oceanarium in Hong Kong where they lived only a short time. Reports of the behavior of Fraser's dolphins are sketchy. For the most part they are very wary of ships and swim rapidly away when approached, which may very well account for their relative obscurity. They are sighted relatively frequently in the eastern tropical Pacific Ocean because of extensive cetacean research in the area.

Physical description: This is a stocky animal with a short but well-defined beak.

Color: Gray dorsally, white ventrally, with gray flippers. A thick dark stripe appears on most animals below a cream-colored stripe, both extending along lower flanks from rostrum to anus. Dark gray sides of the lower jaw lighten gradually toward the flippers.

Fins and flukes: A tiny, dark gray, falcate dorsal fin is located on the midback region. Tiny flippers are thin and curve to points. Small, well-developed flukes are pointed or slightly rounded at their tips, with a small median notch.

Length and weight: These animals reach at least 2.4 m (8 ft) and an estimated weight of 64 to 82 kg (140 to 180 lb).

Teeth: Each side of the upper jaw contains 40 to 44 small, conical teeth; the lower has 39 to 44 per side.

Feeding: Stomach contents contained deep-sea fish, squid, and crustaceans.

Breathing and diving: No information is available.

Mating and breeding: No information is available.

Herding: They herd in large numbers, often more than 500. In the eastern tropical Pacific Ocean they often swim in close proximity to spinner (page 128) and spotted dolphins (page 135), striped dolphins (page 138), false killer whales (page 172), and sperm whales (page 84).

Robert Pitman

Distribution: Known to inhabit the eastern tropical Pacific, the Indo-Pacific region, and recent reports put them in the tropical Atlantic. Strandings have occurred in Australia, South Africa, and Japan.

Migration: No information is available.

Above, a pod of Fraser's dolphins reveal the tiny flippers, flukes, and dorsal fins typical of this species. Note also the ill-defined beak and dark stripe usually found along each flank.

Right, inhabiting the Atlantic and Pacific Oceans in large herds, Fraser's dolphins are usually shy animals and will swim rapidly away from boats.

WHITE-BEAKED DOLPHIN

Family **Delphinidae**
Genus ***Lagenorhynchus***
Species ***L. albirostris*** (Gray, 1846)

Common names can be misleading: In some geographic areas this animal has a gray beak, or even a dark one. It is the northernmost member of a worldwide genus; although it is fairly common, no white-beaked dolphin has ever been kept in captivity successfully and little is known about it.

White-beaked dolphins are such fast swimmers that they create a "rooster tail" wake as do Dall's porpoises (page 214). They do not ride bow-waves of vessels.

Physical description: A very stocky body with a small but distinct beak is characteristic.

Color: Dorsal region is dark gray from beak demarcation to and including tail, converging to lighter gray flanks and white ventral region. Upper and lower rostrum areas are usually white but can be dark. Flippers and flukes are entirely dark. Each flank displays a poorly defined white stripe from just below the dorsal fin to the lower peduncle. Dull white also is visible from just behind the dorsal fin extending down the dorsal ridge to disappear into dark gray at the tail.

Fins and flukes: The falcate dorsal fin is tall and prominent. Medium-sized flippers are very well defined and pointed at the tips. Flukes are pointed at the tips, with a definite median notch.

Length and weight: This dolphin reaches 3 m (10 ft) and an estimated 227 to 272 kg (500 to 600 lb).

Teeth: 22 to 28 small, conical teeth are found in each side of the upper and lower jaws.

Feeding: Known to feed on squid, cod, herring, octopus, capelin, and small crustaceans.

Breathing and diving: No information is available.

Mating and breeding: Calves are born at about 114 cm (3.75 ft) and 40 kg (88 lb), probably between June and September. They are quite large, probably because of birth into cold water, which requires a thick blubber layer. Sexual maturity is reached at about 1.95 m (6.5 ft).

Lee Tepley

Herding: Observed in herds as large as 1,500 individuals; groups of 6 to 10 are quite common.

Distribution: Restricted to the coastal regions of the North Atlantic Ocean from New England east to the Barents Sea and the North Sea.

Migration: There may be a migration to Davis Strait in spring and late autumn, with a southern movement in the winter evidently as far as Cape Cod, Massachusetts, where they may remain until the early spring or summer months.

Richard Sears, MICS

Left, taken from movie footage, this picture is the only underwater shot in existence of a free-swimming white-beaked dolphin.

Above, white-beaked dolphins have an extremely limited distribution in the western North Atlantic and are rarely photographed.

ATLANTIC WHITE-SIDED DOLPHIN

Family **Delphinidae**
Genus *Lagenorhynchus*
Species *L. acutus*   (Gray, 1828)

This strikingly patterned dolphin can be identified by the short, thick stripe on each side of the peduncle, which ranges in color from tan to yellow. Atlantic white-sided dolphins are often found in very large herds of up to a thousand individuals, subdivided into pods of 2 to 5 animals. They are avid bow-wave riders and often leap clear of the water as they swim.

Physical description: Small, poorly demarcated beak. The body is very much like that of the white-beaked dolphin (page 144).

Color: The entire dorsal region is black, from tip of upper jaw to flukes. This dark region continues from the juncture of the tail and peduncle toward the head, tapering away midway to the dorsal fin. A thin black line extends from the demarcation of the beak to a circular patch around each eye. Lower flanks are gray from just before the eyes to just past the anus, where two lines meet to encompass the remainder of the underside. Ventral regions are white from the lower jaw to just past the anus. A barely discernible dark streak runs from each eye to the leading margins of the flippers. Within the gray on each flank, a yellowish white patch begins just below the dorsal fin and extends halfway back on the peduncle—this is probably the animal's most distinctive characteristic.

Fins and flukes: The falcate dorsal fin is very tall and pointed at the tip. Thin flippers are well-developed and pointed. Flukes are well spread, with a small median notch.

Length and weight: It reaches 3 m (10 ft) and 190 to 250 kg (420 to 550 lb).

Teeth: Each side of the upper and lower jaws contains 30 to 34 small, sharp, conical teeth.

Feeding: Known to feed on shrimp, smelt, hake, squid, and herring.

Breathing and diving: No information is available.

Right, this inquisitive Atlantic white-sided dolphin approached the diver repeatedly.

Opposite, often traveling in groups of up to a thousand animals, the Atlantic white-sided dolphin can be identified by the yellowish white stripe on its peduncle.

Richard Sears, MICS

Mating and breeding: A 107 to 122 cm (42 to 48 in) calf is born in spring or midsummer after a 10-month gestation period. Lactation lasts for 18 months; calving occurs every two or three years.

Herding: Usually groups of 10 to 60 when inshore of its range; herds up to 1,000 have been observed at sea.

Distribution: North Atlantic Ocean from Massachusetts and southern Greenland, east to western Norway and the British Isles.

Migration: No information is available.

Natural history notes: Individual and mass strandings are quite common; these are the most commonly stranded small whales in the New England region of the United States. They are thought to live to at least 27 years.

PACIFIC WHITE-SIDED DOLPHIN

Family **Delphinidae**
Genus *Lagenorhynchus*
Species *L. obliquidens*   Gill, 1865

Like its Atlantic counterpart, the Pacific white-sided dolphin is marked by soft, subtle color patterns. At sea it often leaps from the water, cavorting, gamboling, and seeming to do nearly anything to make a splash. These animals are avid bow-wave riders. Pacific white-sided dolphins are normally deep-water inhabitants; surprisingly, they do very well in captivity.

Right, avid bow-wave riders, Pacific white-sided dolphins may form large herds and create a spectacular disturbance when accompanying large ships.

Physical description: Beak poorly demarcated.

Color: Dorsal area is soft black extending to and including flukes. The beak is black, extending to include the eyes. Flippers and dorsal fin are black blending to white on their trailing margins. The flanks are gray with a thin white stripe from the sides of the peduncle extending up the dorsal region to the end of the forehead.

Fins and flukes: The dorsal fin is large, falcate, and rounded; more pointed and triangular and less falcate in the young. Flippers are small, well defined, and rounded at tips. Flukes are very well developed, with a median notch.

Length and weight: The Pacific white-sided dolphin reaches 2.1 to 2.4 m (7 to 8 ft) and at least 150 kg (330 lb).

Teeth: 23 to 33 small, conical teeth are found in each side of the upper and lower jaws.

Feeding: Hake, anchovy, squid, herring, and sardine.

Breathing and diving: No information is available.

Mating and breeding: Mating and calving season is during summer and early fall. The 80 to 94 cm (31 to 37 in) calves are born after a 12-month gestation period.

Herding: Up to 1,000, in groups up to 40. Ordinarily homogeneous, they are nonetheless often found with striped dolphins (page 138), common dolphins (page 140), and northern right whale dolphins (page 162).

Distribution: North Pacific Ocean. They frequent the waters off the coast of North America from southeastern Alaska to Baja California; off the coast of Asia from the Kuril Islands to Japan.

Migration: Apparently north in spring; south in autumn, within their range.

Robert Pitman

Left, although they are normally open-ocean animals, Pacific white-sided dolphins endure captivity surprisingly well.

Below, all six species of *Lagenorhynchus,* the genus to which Pacific white-sided dolphins belong, are characterized by large, well-defined fins and flukes, striking color patterns, and a barely discernible beak.

Stanley M. Minasian

Stanley M. Minasian

DUSKY DOLPHIN

Family **Delphinidae**
Genus **Lagenorhynchus**
Species **L. obscurus** (Gray, 1828)

Taxonomic note: Some populations displaying slight color variations are occasionally referred to as *Lagenorhynchus fitzroyi* and called Fitzroy's dolphin, although this is not officially recognized.

Despite the fact that the populations are widely separated, the dusky dolphin's color pattern bears a striking resemblance to that of the Pacific white-sided dolphin (page 148). Some researchers have attempted to bunch all *Lagenorhynchus* found in the Pacific Ocean (Pacific white-sided, Peale's, and dusky dolphins) into one species, *Lagenorhynchus obliquidens*. This has met with a great deal of resistance, for although the species look remarkably alike, they are apparently different in ways other than color and minor physical disparities.

Dusky dolphins are extremely inquisitive animals which seem to enjoy the company of ships and divers in their waters.

Physical description: The dusky dolphin's physique is very similar to that of Peale's dolphin (page 152) and the Pacific white-sided dolphin (page 148). A prominent ridge runs from the dorsal fin to the flukes.

Color: Blue and white. A beautiful turquoise dorsal region runs from a small but discernible beak to and including the flukes and drops longitudinally across the upper flanks. The ventral region is white with a thin light stripe extending from the lower peduncle area across the upper flanks to dissolve near the blowhole. A bold white stripe runs from the ventral area into the blue region, then to just under the dorsal fin where it tapers out sharply. Leading edges of flippers fade from blue to white on their posterior edges. In most, the eyes and tips of jaws are dark.

Fins and flukes: A large falcate dorsal fin is well-developed. Flippers are well spread and nearly pointed at the tips. Flukes are small and pointed at their tips, with a median notch.

Length and weight: Average length is 1.4 m (4.5 ft), weight about 136 kg (300 lb). The largest recorded animal was 2 m (6.75 ft). Males are slightly larger than females.

Teeth: There are 24 to 36 small, conical teeth in each side of the upper and lower jaws.

Feeding: Known to feed on squid and small fish such as anchovies.

Breathing and diving: The behavior of Argentine animals is markedly different during evening and daylight hours. Slow, lethargic swimming and breathing are typical during the evening; daytime patterns show much more activity, no doubt because the animals are feeding.

Mating and breeding: The gestation period is 9 to 11 months. Calves of New Zealand herds reportedly are born in midwinter; in Argentina birthing takes place in the summer months. Lactation lasts about 18 months. Calving intervals are 2 to 3 years.

Herding: Normally 5 to 30, but herds up to several hundred are quite common. It has been suggested that herds form on an age-group basis.

Distribution: Apparent circumpolar distribution in cool temperate inshore waters off South America, South Africa, Kerguelen Island, Campbell Island, southern Australia, and New Zealand.

Migration: Australian and New Zealand animals appear to migrate to northern New Zealand in April to mate and calve, and return to extreme southern waters in October and November. South African populations migrate progressively as far north as Walvis Bay, returning to the Southern Hemisphere in October and November.

Dusky dolphins are probably the easiest to approach of all the small cetaceans. Also extremely active, they often somersault high out of the water.

Marc Webber

Left, dusky dolphins will travel for miles to ride the bow-waves of ships passing through their native waters.

Below, so closely do dusky dolphins resemble Pacific white-sided dolphins that some scientists suggest that they are the same species, varying by region.

Robert Pitman

Stephen Leatherwood

PEALE'S DOLPHIN

Family **Delphinidae**
Genus *Lagenorhynchus*
Species *L. australis* (Peale, 1848)

As is true for many cetaceans inhabiting remote parts of the Southern Hemisphere, observation and good photographs of Peale's dolphin are rare. Only about 20 specimens of Peale's dolphin are known, and little is known about its external characteristics or its behavior.

Physical description: Very similar to the Pacific white-sided dolphin (page 148).

Color: Dorsal region is black from forehead to anus; a barely discernible beak is black from eyes to tip of snout. Sides of the underchin are black. The throat is white. Flanks are light gray with black flippers. A distinct light-gray-to-white demarcation from eyes to flippers ends at the flanks just behind the dorsal fin. The dorsal region is dark from the beak to and including the flukes. A sharply defined white patch in the peduncle region stretches forward to just below the dorsal fin, where a continuing white line runs into the dark region, up to the blowhole, then fades.

Fins and flukes: The large dorsal fin is well-defined and falcate. Small flippers are thin and pointed. Flukes are very well developed and pointed at their tips, with a median notch.

Length and weight: This animal reaches 2.1 m (7 ft) and about 136 kg (300 lb).

Teeth: 30 small, conical teeth are found in each side of the upper and lower jaws.

Feeding: One specimen had octopus remains in its stomach.

Breathing and diving: No information is available.

Mating and breeding: Little is known. Calves were observed in the Chilean Strait of Magellan in January and February of 1984. They had adult color patterns with slightly muted gray tones.

Herding: The herds average 30 but can exceed 100, broken into groups of 3 to 10. Peale's dolphins have been observed playing in surf waves with Risso's dolphins (page 166).

Distribution: Temperate waters of the Pacific and Atlantic oceans off southern South America and the Falkland Islands.

Migration: No information is available.

Natural history notes: These animals do occasionally ride bow-waves and have been observed playing near vessels as long as the vessel remained within the confines of kelp beds.

Ron Kastelein

This Peale's dolphin approached a research ship off southern Chile, providing a very rare photographic opportunity.

Left, taken off southern Chile, this photograph reveals the color pattern of the elusive Peale's dolphin.

Illustrated *below,* the little understood Peale's dolphin is found off southern South America and the Falkland Islands.

Stephen Leatherwood

Illustrated by Larry A. Foster

LF

HOURGLASS DOLPHIN

Family **Delphinidae**
Genus **Lagenorhynchus**
Species **L. cruciger** (Quoy and Gaimard, 1824)

Taxonomic note: Animals with slight size and color variations are wrongly referred to as *Lagenorhynchus wilsoni* and are called Wilson's hourglass dolphins.

The hourglass dolphin resides in a little-traveled part of the circumpolar regions of the Antarctic. As with some other cetaceans that live their entire lives in remote areas, study of the animal is difficult, and little is known about it.

Left, **inhabitants of remote subant-arctic and antarctic seas, hourglass dolphins are rarely encountered and little known.**

Opposite, **a rare whole-body photograph of leaping hourglass dolphins, named for the white hourglass-shaped pattern on their flanks.**

Peter C. Beamish

Physical description: Stocky body. Small but well-defined rostrum.

Color: Black on the rostrum extends dorsally to the tips of the flukes. Lower flanks, including flippers and flukes are also black. The ventral region is white from chin to caudal peduncle. Dark dorsal and ventral areas extend and touch on flanks just below the dorsal fin creating a unique hourglass shape.

Fins and flukes: Very tall, prominent, falcate dorsal fin. Long, curved flippers are pointed at their tips. Well-defined flukes are slightly rounded at the tips, with a median notch.

Length and weight: Little is known, but a 1.6 m (5.25 ft) male and a 1.8 m (6 ft) female have been recorded. The female weighed 114 kg (250 lb).

Teeth: About 28 small, conical teeth are found in each side of the upper and lower jaws.

Feeding: No information is available.

Breathing and diving: They have a smooth, undulating motion when swimming, like a group of penguins.

Mating and breeding: No information is available.

Herding: Groups of 2 to 4 seem normal, but one herd of about 40 has been sighted.

Distribution: A pelagic species found in the temperate waters of South Atlantic and South Pacific oceans.

Migration: No information is available.

Natural history notes: These animals are known to ride bow-waves, making fast, high leaps as they approach a ship.

COMMERSON'S DOLPHIN

Family **Delphinidae**
Genus *Cephalorhynchus*
Species ***C. commersonii*** (Lacépède, 1804)

Like the other three members of the genus *Cephalorhynchus* (Chilean dolphin [page 159], Heaviside's dolphin [page 158], and Hector's dolphin [page 160]), Commerson's dolphin inhabits waters of the Southern Hemisphere exclusively, and little is known about it. Also like the other members of its genus, Commerson's dolphin has a short, rounded dorsal fin, rounded, paddle-shaped flippers, and flukes wider than might be expected for an animal of its size. The appearance of its face closely resembles that of the harbor porpoise (page 206).

Physical description: Small and stocky, resembling a fat harbor porpoise. The small, underdeveloped rostrum does not protrude.

Color: Head, neck, flippers, and flukes are black and distinctly separated from the snow-white dorsal region which extends from the forehead back past the dorsal fin and on either flank to the underside just past the large black patch on the anus. Black begins again along the dorsal ridge running down the sides of the peduncle including the dorsal fin and entire fluke region.

Fins and flukes: The prominent, rounded dorsal fin meets a slight dorsal ridge as it falls to the rear. The ridge runs halfway down the peduncle with little or no discernible falcation in the dorsal fin itself. Small flippers are rounded on their leading edges and tips. The small flukes are crescent shaped, rounded at tips, with a well-defined median notch.

Length and weight: Adults reach 1.6 m (5.25 ft).

Teeth: 29 to 30 small conical teeth are found in each side of upper and lower jaws.

Feeding: Krill, cuttlefish, squid, shrimp, and small fish.

Breathing and diving: Commerson's dolphins are often seen swimming in the bow-wake of passing ships. Their normal diving time is 15 to 20 seconds; swimming speed 10 to 13.5 kmph (7 to 8.5 mph).

Mating and breeding: Study of fetuses suggest calving in early austral summer. Young are born all brown and develop adult markings with age.

Roy Manston

Herding: Individually, or in small groups from 6 to 30. A herd of about 100 was once sighted.

Distribution: Southern tip of South America, Strait of Magellan, Tierra del Fuego, Falkland Islands, South Georgia, and Kerguelen Island.

Migration: No information is available.

Natural history notes: These animals are extremely active, observations report repeated high leaps from the water. Their swimming pattern is erratic, making it difficult to tell where they will surface next. At the time of this writing, five of these animals are in captivity at Sea World in San Diego, California.

Stephen Leatherwood

Opposite, this Commerson's dolphin was one of five caught in the South Atlantic for shipment to a Japanese marine park. Confiscated en route in the United States for violation of the Marine Mammal Protection Act, all five animals subsequently died as a result of their capture.

Above, avid bow-wave riders, Commerson's dolphins inhabit the lonely waters around eastern Tierra del Fuego, the Falkland Islands, South Georgia, and Kerguelen Island in the Indian Ocean.

157

HEAVISIDE'S DOLPHIN

Family **Delphinidae**
Genus *Cephalorhynchus*
Species *C. heavisidii* (Gray, 1828)

Although it was first described more than a century and a half ago, information about this small dolphin is still almost nonexistent. It, too, lives in a remote area, and is shy and retiring by habit. Until recently there has been no serious effort to study the animal. All descriptions have been taken from less than a dozen dead specimens and from drawings made by persons who observed them. The dolphin was named in the early 1800s by a Captain Haviside, who collected natural history specimens from the Cape of Good Hope. (His name was misspelled when it was given to the dolphin.)

Illustrated by Larry A. Foster

Physical description: Body closely resembles that of Hector's dolphin (page 160), except that the dorsal fin is triangular, the beak is less extended, and the slightly rounded flippers are smaller.

Color: Similar to Hector's dolphin except that the white on the Heaviside's posterior ventral region continues along the flanks to the throat, divided only by a thin line extending from the dark dorsal area to the leading margin of the flippers.

Length and weight: Reaches a known length of 1.2 to 1.3 m (4 to 4.25 ft), and an estimated 45 kg (100 lb).

Teeth: 25 to 30 small, sharp teeth are located in each side of the upper and lower jaws.

Feeding: Squid and bottom-dwelling fish.

Breathing and diving: No information is available.

Mating and breeding: No information is available.

Herding: Unknown; thought to be very small.

Distribution: Coastal waters from Cape of Good Hope north to Cape Cross, Southwest Africa.

Migration: No information is available.

Little known because of its remote distribution and shy nature, Heaviside's dolphin, illustrated here, is found in the coastal waters off the Cape of Good Hope north to Cape Cross, Southwest Africa.

CHILEAN DOLPHIN

black dolphin

Family **Delphinidae**
Genus *Cephalorhynchus*
Species ***C. eutropia*** (Gray, 1846)

Not only does the Chilean dolphin reside exclusively in a remote area off the coast of Chile, it is also a shy species and avoids ships, making even simple observation difficult. It has a stocky body, rounded dorsal fin and flippers, and is white ventrally, but in general its color pattern is not as dramatic as the others of its genus.

Little is known about the Chilean dolphin, illustrated here, though its color pattern appears to be less dramatic than others in its genus.

Illustrated by Larry A. Foster

Physical description: Closely resembles Commerson's dolphin (page 156) except that it shows much darker gray patches of white along the throat, behind the flippers, and on the belly region.

Color: Dark dorsally overall, with a white throat and belly region. White spots behind the flippers. A light gray patch extends from the tip of the snout to the blowhole.

Length and weight: Reaches at least 1.2 m (4 ft) and an estimated 54 kg (119 lb).

Teeth: 28 to 31 conical teeth in each side of upper and lower jaws.

Feeding: Known to feed on cuttlefish and shrimp.

Breathing and diving: No information is available.

Mating and breeding: No information is available.

Herding: Rare sightings suggest these animals swim alone or in groups of up to a dozen.

Distribution: Found only along the southern coast of Chile from Concepción to Isla Navarino and Tierra del Fuego.

Migration: No information is available.

HECTOR'S DOLPHIN

Family **Delphinidae**
Genus *Cephalorhynchus*
Species *C. hectori* (van Beneden, 1881)

Taxonomic note: Some researchers refer to animals with slight color variations as *Cephalorhynchus albifrons*.

Hector's dolphin inhabits the turbid coastal waters of New Zealand, where groups of 3 to 10 individuals gather at a time, swimming among the surf-lashed rocks close to shore. This beautiful, poorly known animal's color pattern closely resembles that of the killer whale (page 178). Some individuals have been kept in captivity; they were listless and seemed uncomfortable at first, but when their water was made slightly cloudy (conforming to their habitat in the wild) they responded favorably, settling down and becoming more responsive.

Physical description: The body is fairly stocky with a barely discernible beak.

Color: Tip of lower jaw and sides of the head region are black leading to and including flippers. Dorsal region and flanks are light brown. Ventral area is white from lower chin to anus, sharply delineated from the dark dorsal regions. White branches up on the lower peduncle area, sweeping sharply back toward the peduncle where it tapers to an end. Lower flanks are lighter than surrounding regions from the flippers to the white ventral extensions—a distinction sometimes barely visible but defined by a longitudinal line across the flanks. The anal region displays a color pattern that distinguishes males from females. Males have a single dark spot on the anus, females have more than one. Dark flank regions extend under the body at the flippers to touch and extend back to an abruptly tapered end.

Fins and flukes: The black dorsal fin is very rounded and tilted toward the rear. Very dark flippers are large and paddle shaped. Dark flukes are disproportionately elongated and pointed at their tips, with a definite median notch.

Length and weight: Hector's dolphin reaches 1.5 to 1.8 m (5 to 6 ft) and 54 kg (120 lb).

Teeth: 30 to 32 small, conical teeth are found in each side of upper and lower jaws.

Feeding: Stomach contents from 2 specimens contained small quantities of shellfish, crustaceans, small fish, and squid.

Breathing and diving: No information is available.

Mating and breeding: Calves are believed to be born during December-January migration.

Herding: Usually seen in groups of 3 to 10; larger herds, up to several hundred, have been observed.

Distribution: Coastal waters of New Zealand. Also reported near Australia and believed to occur in Sarawak, Borneo. It does not avoid muddy or turbid waters, and will enter estuarine waters of the Clarence, Gray, and Wanganui rivers of New Zealand.

Migration: Generally believed to migrate to North Island, New Zealand, in December and January, and return to South Island in February.

Natural history notes: This animal prefers to ride the wake rather than the bow-wave of passing ships. It is not known to expose much of its body as it swims and occasionally leaps from the water.

Mother and calf Hector's dolphins in Cook Strait, New Zealand, show the light color typical of these animals in the muddy or turbid water they inhabit. In captivity the animal's skin becomes darker since the clear water where they are kept allows far greater exposure to the sun.

William Dawbin

William Dawbin

Left, Hector's dolphin is easily recognized by its rounded dorsal fin, lack of a discernible beak, and complex three-toned color pattern.

Below, listless at first in captivity, Hector's dolphins became more responsive when their water was made cloudy to resemble their natural habitat.

William Dawbin

NORTHERN RIGHT WHALE DOLPHIN

Family **Delphinidae**
Genus *Lissodelphis*
Species *L. borealis* (Peale, 1848)

Taxonomic note: Animals with slight color variations found in the waters around Japan are occasionally referred to as *Lissodelphis borealis albiventris*, a subspecies, although this claim is neither widely recognized nor accepted.

Physically, this animal represents an extreme in aquatic adaptation. While most dolphins have a prominent dorsal fin, fair-sized flippers, and, in general, present a full-bodied appearance, the northern right whale dolphin is the slenderest of all cetaceans and lacks any semblance of a dorsal fin. Its sleekness befits its style of traveling in long, low leaps that only slightly disturb the surrounding water. Primarily black, this animal has a hard-edged, pure white area covering its chest and extend-

ing ventrally in a thin white line to its flukes (the white line at the genitals is wider in females than in males). There are many slight color variations within the herds.

As is the case with several other cetacean species, the common name is misleading, for apart from the absence of a dorsal fin it bears no resemblance whatsoever to its namesake, the right whale (page 72), and most researchers refer to it simply as *Lissodelphis*.

Physical description: The lower jaw extends slightly ahead of the upper jaw. This is the sleekest of all cetaceans.

Color: This animal is almost completely black but for the chest and underside, already described. Normally, the animals have a white patch in the vicinity of the lower jaw. The underside of the flukes is white from the tips to near the center. The undersides of the flippers, and occasionally the upper sides as well, are white.

Fins and flukes: There is no dorsal fin. The small, well-developed flippers are rounded along the leading margins and nearly pointed at the tips. The flukes are very small comparatively, rounded at the tips, with a slight median notch.

Length and weight: The largest male recorded reached 3 m (10 ft) in length; the largest female, 2.3 m (7.5 ft). They reach a weight of about 82 kg (180 lb).

Teeth: They possess 37 to 43 small, sharply pointed teeth in each side of the upper jaw; 40 to 46 in each side of the lower jaw.

Feeding: They are known to feed on squid and pelagic fish.

Breathing and diving: No information is available.

Mating and breeding: Calves of 60 to 70 cm (24 to 28 in) reportedly are born in April and May and are much lighter in color than adults. Males reach sexual maturity at about 2.1 m (7 ft); females at about 1.98 m (6.5 ft).

Herding: They have been observed in groups of up to 2,000 animals.

Distribution: They are found throughout the temperate waters of the North Pacific Ocean from Japan and the Kurile Islands to British Columbia and Baja California.

Migration: They frequent southern California waters from October or November until April. Western North Pacific populations migrate south in autumn or winter to near the southern Kurile Islands.

Natural history notes: Avid bow-wave riders, these dolphins often make long, low leaps clear of the water as they swim. They are known to associate closely or swim with pilot whales (page 174), Risso's dolphins (page 166), Pacific white-sided dolphins (page 148), common dolphins (page 140), sei whales (page 50), humpback whales (page 56), gray whales (page 64), and California sea lions.

Taken from the bow of a speeding ship, this photograph catches a northern right whale dolphin at a favorite activity—bow-wave riding.

Robert Pitman

Robert Pitman

Lissome northern right whale dolphins swim together in the clear waters of the north Pacific Ocean.

SOUTHERN RIGHT WHALE DOLPHIN

Family **Delphinidae**
Genus *Lissodelphis*
Species ***L. peronii***   (Lacépède, 1804)

The southern right whale dolphin differs sufficiently from its northern counterpart to earn classification as a distinct species within the genus. Although this animal also is long and slender, the white pigmentation that forms a thin, elegant line along the ventral surface in the northern right whale dolphin becomes enlarged here, entirely covering the southern animal's lower flanks. The southern animal's forehead and beak are also white, and—an unusual feature among cetaceans—the dorsal surface of the flippers is often white as well.

Several sightings of these rare animals have confirmed that they swim in large herds.

The graceful southern right whale dolphin displays much more white than does its northern cousin.

Keiji Naso, Courtesy Masahara Nishiwaki

Peter Harper, Courtesy Alan Baker, National Museum of New Zealand

Physical description: Somewhat smaller than the northern right whale dolphin (page 162), with a stouter rostrum.

Color: Anterior flanks are black; the dorsal region is black from just past the demarcation of the rostrum to and including the flukes. Ventral regions are a well-defined gray to white from the rostrum past and including the flippers down into the lower peduncle region, ending at the beginning of the flukes. The underside of the flukes is white with a black border.

Fins and flukes: No dorsal fin. Small, well-developed flippers are rounded toward body and nearly pointed at their tips. Flukes are small—rounded at the tips, with a well-defined median notch.

Length and weight: Southern right whale dolphins reach about 1.8 to 2.4 m (6 to 8 ft) and 68 kg (150 lb).

Teeth: 43 to 47 small, sharply pointed teeth are found in each side of upper and lower jaws.

Feeding: Pelagic fish and squid.

Breathing and diving: No information is available.

Mating and breeding: No information is available.

Herding: Normally 2 to 50. Sightings around St. Paul's Island confirm herds as large as 1,000. South American herds associate, but do not mingle, with *Lagenorhynchus* species in the same waters.

Distribution: This wholly pelagic species inhabits the temperate and subantarctic waters of the South Pacific Ocean, the Tasman Sea, and waters directly south of Australia.

Migration: No information is available.

Living in remote waters of the South Pacific Ocean and Tasman Sea, the southern right whale dolphin's forehead, beak, and flippers' dorsal surface are white, unusual for cetaceans.

RISSO'S DOLPHIN
grampus

Family **Delphinidae**
Genus *Grampus*
Species *G. griseus*   (G. Cuvier, 1812)

One of the larger dolphins, Risso's dolphin is stocky from its head to its large dorsal fin; thereafter its body tapers quickly giving the animal an unusual profile. Risso's may be a peculiarly aggressive or territorial dolphin; the animals' bodies are often covered with scratches that match the pattern of their teeth. The dolphin known as Pelorus Jack was probably a Risso's dolphin.

Between 1888 and 1912 this dolphin faithfully accompanied ships crossing Cook Strait at Pelorus Sound between New Zealand's two main islands. On one occasion someone shot at Jack from a ferry boat, and he disappeared for about six months. When the dolphin reappeared he resumed guiding ships—except that ferry—across the strait.

Physical description: The stocky body becomes slender behind the dorsal fin. The large melon is divided by a vertical indentation running down the forehead almost to the mouth. The beak is not visible.

Color: Dark gray with light gray patches on ventral region. Juveniles are light gray. Older males often show white scarring all over the body, presumably from confrontations with other Risso's dolphins; scarring increases with age and some individuals are almost entirely white from it.

Fins and flukes: The tall, prominent dorsal fin, situated at the midback region, grows to 38 cm (15 in) and is falcate and rounded at its tip. Flippers and flukes are long and pointed; flukes have a definite median notch.

Length and weight: Risso's dolphin reaches 4.3 m (14 ft) and 680 kg (1,500 lb).

Teeth: Teeth are absent in the upper jaw; lower jaw contains 3 to 7 large, conical teeth per side.

Feeding: Primarily cephalopods; also small fish.

Breathing and diving: Risso's dolphins have a barely discernible blow and often make spectacular twisting and rolling leaps from the water as they swim. They also raise their head above the water when swimming with small boats.

Mating and breeding: Calves are 1.5 m (5 ft) long at birth, becoming sexually mature at about 3 m (10 ft).

Herding: Herds from 5 to several hundred animals have been observed.

Distribution: Worldwide in tropical and temperate seas.

Migration: Seasonal North Atlantic migrations to higher latitudes have been suggested.

Natural history notes: Risso's dolphins have been observed in the presence of northern right whale dolphins (page 162) and short-finned pilot whales (page 176). They prefer deep-water regions. Risso's dolphins are believed to live to at least 20 years of age.

Opposite, Risso's dolphins are among the largest of the dolphins and are rapid swimmers. This individual eyed the photographer.

Below, Risso's dolphins are distinguished by robust body, markedly thin tail stock, and a vertical crease on the melon.

David K. Caldwell

MELON-HEADED WHALE

Family **Delphinidae**
Genus *Peponocephala*
Species *P. electra*   (Gray, 1846)

When first described by Gray in 1846, the melon-headed whale was thought to be a member of the genus *Lagenorhynchus*. Since that time, however, no other specimen of *Lagenorhynchus* has been found that fits Gray's description. In 1966, the animal was studied in Hawaii and placed in the genus *Peponocephala*, of which it is the only member. These dolphins once were thought rare, but sizeable populations have been observed near the Philippines and in the waters of Hawaii and Japan. In captivity they seem to incite fear reactions in other dolphins. At sea from a distance they are very difficult to distinguish from pygmy killer whales (page 170).

Howard Hall, Living Ocean Society

Left, melon-headed whales form large herds numbering several hundred individuals.

Right, often confused with the pygmy killer whale, the melon-headed whale characteristically has pointed flippers while the other's are wider and round at the tips.

Physical description: These animals have a slight indentation above the sides of the upper jaw, similar to that of false killer whales (page 172) and pygmy killer whales (page 170), but there is no discernible beak. The tips of the upper and lower jaws are practically even, whereas the upper jaw obviously overhangs the lower in the pygmy killer whale.

Color: Dark gray over the entire body. The slightly darker saddle on the back extends down the sides from just forward of the dorsal fin. A thin white strip runs along the upper and lower lips, and a white anchor pattern appears on the upper chest.

Fins and flukes: The prominent dorsal fin is large, falcate, and located halfway down the back. Flippers are sickle-shaped, curved along the leading margins and pointed at the tips. Flukes are well-developed, pointed or slightly rounded at the tips, with a definite median notch.

Length and weight: These animals reach at least 2.6 m (8 ft) and 182 kg (400 lb).

Teeth: 21 to 25 small, pointed teeth are found in each side of upper and lower jaws.

Feeding: Known to feed on squid and small fish.

Breathing and diving: They are known to jump completely clear of the water as they swim and to ride the bow-waves of ships.

Mating and breeding: Animals with newborn have been reported in the Southern Hemisphere during July and August, suggesting spring breeding.

Herding: They are known to herd in numbers of between 300 and 500.

Distribution: Tropical and temperate Atlantic, Indian, and Pacific oceans.

Migration: No information is available.

PYGMY KILLER WHALE

Family **Delphinidae**
Genus *Feresa*
Species *F. attenuata* Gray, 1874

At sea the pygmy killer whale is often mistaken for the similar melon-headed whale (page 168). It is, however, a smaller dolphin with relatively large, rounded flippers somewhat like those of the killer whale from which it takes its name.

Although most dolphins feed almost exclusively on fish and squid, there have been unconfirmed reports of pygmy killer whales attacking other species of dolphins.

In captivity this animal has displayed a marked aggressiveness toward humans and provoked fear reactions in other dolphins. One particular specimen, kept alive for several weeks at Sea Life Park in Hawaii, behaved aggressively from the moment of its capture, taking every opportunity to snap at anyone within its range. After it became accustomed to captivity it allowed divers to enter its tank, but warned them against approaching too closely by snapping its jaws repeatedly.

Observations both in captivity and in the wild show that this animal has the ability to extend its eyes out from the sockets to look behind itself. Although pygmy killer whales are avid bow-wave riders, they maintain their distance from divers who attempt to approach them underwater.

Al Giddings, Ocean Images, Inc.

Left, this pygmy killer whale approached the photographer in the clear waters off Hawaii and remained close to him for over an hour.

Opposite, the pygmy killer whale's characteristic white lips are clearly visible in this photograph taken from a ship's underwater observation port.

Physical description: Very similar to the melon-headed whale with only subtle visible physical differences. The upper jaw overhangs the lower by several centimeters.

Color: Dark dorsal region; the ventral regions may be dark, matching the dorsal regions, or may be lighter, depending on the individual. The ridges, at least, of both jaws are white.

Fins and flukes: The large, triangular dorsal fin is slightly falcate. Flippers are proportionally large,

Robert Pitman

paddle-shaped, and rounded much like those of the killer whale. Flukes are well-defined and rounded at their tips, with a definite median notch.

Length and weight: The pygmy killer whale reaches 2.1 to 2.4 m (7 to 8 ft) and exceeds 160 kg (350 lb).

Teeth: 10 to 13 are found in each side of upper and lower jaws.

Feeding: The diet includes squid and small fish.

Breathing and diving: Although the individuals of a herd are often observed submerging and rising in unison, little else is known about their breathing and diving patterns.

Mating and breeding: No information is available.

Herding: A specimen in captivity at Sea Life Park, Hawaii, was taken from a herd of about 50, although herds of several hundred have been observed.

Distribution: Tropical and temperate waters of the Atlantic, Indian, and Pacific oceans.

Migration: No information is available.

Natural history notes: They have been observed swimming with Fraser's dolphins (page 142). In Hawaii they have been seen swimming with humpback whales (page 56).

FALSE KILLER WHALE

Family **Delphinidae**
Genus *Pseudorca*
Species *P. crassidens*　(Owen, 1846)

The false killer whale—one of the largest dolphins—has proven intelligent and responsive in captivity. In the wild it is one of several species known to beach themselves, or strand, in large numbers. The phenomenon of stranding is poorly understood. The act cannot be called suicide, since there is no way to establish that the animals actually plan their own deaths. Some animals, upon being taken out to sea, do come back to shore and certain death; others swim away. Some stranded animals have been found to be heavily infested with parasites, but it is not clear whether such infestation has any relevance to a whale's stranding. Until further research establishes some cause or reason for the phenomenon, almost nothing can be said about it that is not speculative.

In the wild this animal may be confused with the melon-headed whale (page 168), for when swimming on the surface its blunt head and dorsal fins are similar in appearance. However, the false killer whale has a distinct and obvious hump halfway down the leading edge of each flipper, and the body is substantially more elongated.

Physical description: Long, torpedo-shaped body with extended peduncle region. The upper jaw overhangs the lower by several centimeters. The beak is slightly delineated by indentations on either side of the upper jaw.

Color: Glossy black; there may be a medium-gray area from the tip of the lower jaw spreading to the region between the flippers, then tapering off.

Fins and flukes: The dorsal fin is 18 to 41 cm (7 to 16 in) long, located behind the midback region. Flippers have a distinct hump on the leading margin unique to this species that provides easy, positive identification. Flukes are thin and pointed at their tips, with a definite median notch.

Length and weight: Males are 6 m (20 ft) long and weigh about 2,200 kg (4,800 lb); females reach 5 m (16 ft) and an estimated 1,200 kg (2,600 lb).

Teeth: 8 to 11 large, conical teeth are found in each side of the upper and lower jaws.

Feeding: These animals feed extensively on squid and fish up to about 60 cm (24 inches) in length. They have been observed attacking dolphins in the eastern tropical Pacific when they were being released from tuna seining nets.

Breathing and diving: These animals often swim at high speeds, leaping completely out of the water.

Sea Life Park

Above, one of the largest dolphins, the false killer whale is responsive in captivity.

They are avid bow-wave riders and have been observed riding large ground swells.

Mating and breeding: Calves, estimated at 1.8 m (6 ft), are believed to be born at all seasons.

Herding: Usually about 100 animals, sometimes separated into several pods.

Distribution: All temperate and tropical seas.

Migration: No information is available.

Natural history notes: They have been seen swimming with bottlenose dolphins (page 125).

Opposite, the false killer whale is characterized by indentations on each side of the upper lips, a unique bump on the leading edges of the flippers, and the shape of its relatively tall dorsal fin.

LONG-FINNED PILOT WHALE

Family **Delphinidae**
Genus *Globicephala*
Species *G. malaena* (Traill, 1809)

Taxonomic note: The southern population is occasionally referred to as *Globicephala malaena edwardii*, an alleged subspecies. This allegation came about as a result of animals observed with all *Globicephala malaena* characteristics except for shorter flippers.

The long-finned pilot whale is one of the largest cetaceans ever kept in captivity. Whether as a show animal or the subject of exhaustive military experiments, the pilot whale has mastered varied and complex tasks. An extremely friendly animal, it is also one of the most graceful and fluid swimmers when viewed underwater.

Pilot whales were named by European fishermen who believed that herring schools could always be found in the waters beneath the swimming mammals and followed the whales in the hope of catching the fish. They are known to strand in great numbers on beaches, and theories suggest that they follow a single herd leader that, if ill, may beach himself taking the entire herd with him.

Physical description: The body is stocky and extremely elongated, with an exaggerated vertical deepening of the keels at the peduncle. The head is rounded and bulbous with slightly defined lips and little or no discernible beak.

Color: They are jet black with a white anchor-shaped patch on the chin narrowing thinly down the ventral region to the anus.

Fins and flukes: They possess a long, low, falcate dorsal fin located far to the front of the midback region. The flippers are very long and sickle-shaped. The flukes are relatively small, slightly rounded at the tips, with a definite median notch.

Length and weight: Males may exceed 6 m (20 ft) in length and 3,200 kg (7,000 lb); females reach 5.5 m (18 ft) and 3,000 kg (6,500 lb).

Teeth: They have 8 to 10 large, conical teeth nearly 5 cm (2 in) long in each side of the upper and lower jaws.

Feeding: They are known to feed on squid and schooling fish.

Breathing and diving: Pilot whales breathe very quickly, seldom exposing more than the top of the head and the dorsal fin. They are known to dive as deep as 600 m (2,000 ft).

Mating and breeding: Calves of 1.8 m (6 ft) are born after a gestation period of 16 months. Lactation lasts for 20 months. Males reach sexual maturity in 11 years; females in 6.5 years. Birthing apparently takes place every 3 to 5 years and may occur at any time during the year.

Herding: Long-finned pilot whales are gregarious animals herding in very large numbers of up to several hundred individuals.

Distribution: In the Northern Hemisphere they are distributed as far north as Newfoundland, as well as the American and European sides of the temperate Atlantic Ocean. In the Southern Hemisphere, they are found in cool, temperate waters.

Migration: Apparently there is a migration from cold water to warm, but almost nothing is known.

Natural history notes: Males of this species are thought to live 40 years; females between 42 and 50 years.

Courtesy Jim Mullen

Right, in constrast to its short-finned counterpart, the long-finned pilot whale possesses longer, sickle-shaped flippers, and a more elongated dorsal fin positioned farther back on its body.

Opposite, a baby long-finned pilot whale raises its head over its mother to stare at the photographer.

SHORT-FINNED PILOT WHALE

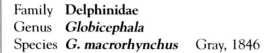

Family **Delphinidae**
Genus *Globicephala*
Species *G. macrorhynchus*   Gray, 1846

Taxonomic note: The southern population is occasionally referred to as *Globicephala scammoni*, either an alleged species or subspecies. It possesses all of the characteristics of the short-finned pilot whale, but has slightly longer flippers.

The animal's bulbous, domelike head is similar to that of the long-finned pilot whale (page 174), as is its exaggerated vertical deepening of the keels at the caudal peduncle. It is distinguished, however, by its uniquely shaped flippers, which appear to be held rigid while the animal swims. As with several other cetacean species, males are larger than females, and have grosser features.

Physical description: Stocky around the midsection, with a very elongated, deep peduncle. The large, rounded head has no beak and slightly defined upper lips.

Color: Jet black with a white anchor-shaped patch on the chin extending down the ventral region to the anus. The anchor patch usually is not present in the variant form.

Fins and flukes: A large, well-defined, falcate dorsal fin stretches back horizontally. Rounded at the top, it is located farther to the front of the midback region than that of any other cetacean. Small, sickle-shaped flippers are well defined. Large, well-developed flukes are widely spread, with a distinct median notch. The variant form possesses longer flippers.

Length and weight: Males reach 5.9 m (19.5 ft) and an estimated 3,000 kg (6,500 lb); females have been recorded slightly exceeding 4 m (13 ft) and about 1,200 kg (2,600 lb).

Teeth: 7 to 9 large, conical teeth are found in each side of the upper and lower jaws. The variant form has 8 to 12 teeth in each side of the upper and lower jaws.

Feeding: Predominantly squid, but small fish are eaten occasionally.

Breathing and diving: Short-finned pilot whales are capable of dives as deep as 600 m (2,000 ft).

Right, **a large group of short-finned pilot whales swim very slowly at the surface.**

Opposite, **a group of short-finned pilot whales in the clear waters of Hawaii. Note the young whale traveling just above the lower animal.**

Robert Pitman

Mating and breeding: The breeding season is thought to be extended; the gestation period is believed to be 11 to 13 months. Calves, 1.4 m (4.5 ft), are born at 3-year intervals.

Herding: Groups of several hundred are common.

Distribution: Tropical and warm, temperate waters of the Atlantic, Pacific, and Indian oceans.

Migration: Definite migration from cold to warm water, but very little is understood.

Natural history notes: They often may be seen "logging" on the surface where they remain stationary, exposing the bulbous head and dorsal fin.

KILLER WHALE

orca

Family **Delphinidae**
Genus *Orcinus*
Species *O. orca* (Linnaeus, 1758)

The killer whale is technically a dolphin, and by far the largest member of that group. Killer whales hunt in packs, and although the bulk of their diet consists of fish and cephalopods such as squid, they also eat seals, sea lions, penguins, dolphins, and porpoises, and have been observed attacking the larger whales, including the blue whale. In both captivity and their natural habitat, they have had ample opportunity to attack humans, yet there is no record of a human death from a killer whale attack. They have a remarkably wide distribution, inhabiting all waters of the world, from polar seas to tropical waters, although they seem most numerous in the Atlantic and Pacific oceans.

The killer whale's pigmentation is striking and varies slightly among herds of different regions. Some males of the Antarctic, for example, have a much larger eye patch than those of other regions. Animals that inhabit Puget Sound show greater variation in shape and pigmentation than populations elsewhere.

The killer whale's social structure is highly evolved. Long-term observations have confirmed regularity in certain habits and feeding patterns. Family units remain intact over long periods, and the underwater vocalizations of killer whales strongly suggest that the animals are always in acoustical communication with one another.

It is interesting that this animal, which for so long has been considered a rapacious marauder of the deep, is in reality capable of gentle, responsive, and sensitive behavior.

Bob Vile, Hubbs–Sea World Research Institute

Left, killer whales attack a blue whale off Cabo San Lucas, Baja California. The blue whale was mortally wounded in the encounter.

Right, found in all waters of the world, the killer whale has a wide distribution. Its striking coloration varies slightly from one geographic area to another.

Kenneth C. Balcomb, III

Physical description: When observed at close range, this long, thick, extremely streamlined animal cannot be mistaken for anything else. The head is bluntly tapered with definite indentations forming the rounded upper lip. The blowhole is located slightly to the left on the forehead. Males are bulkier than females, especially at the head.

Color: Jet black with clearly delineated snow-white regions—white on the underside from the entire lower jaw to the beginning of the flippers, narrowing along the ventral ridge to just past the anus; from just before the anus the white rises as separate patches on both sides curving toward the tail, ending on the dorsal side at about the same point as on the ventral ridge; white in dark regions on each side of the head beginning above the eye and extending back to about the beginning of the flippers. Many individuals have a lighter color pattern just behind the dorsal fin extending asymmetrically to dissolve in dark anterior regions. White areas are yellow-pink in newborns.

Fins and flukes: In males dorsal fins may grow to 1.8 m (6 ft) in height; in females it ceases at 91 cm (3 ft). Flippers are noticeably wider and larger in males than in females. Broad flukes are extremely well-developed, with a definite median notch.

Length and weight: Males are known to reach 9.6 m (31.5 ft) and 8,200 kg (9 tons); females are considerably smaller, reaching 8.2 m (27 ft) and 4,100 kg (4.5 tons).

Teeth: 10 to 12 large, conical teeth are found on each side of the upper and lower jaws. Teeth are slightly curved back and inward.

Feeding: Fish, cephalopods, birds, marine mammals, and sea turtles.

Breathing and diving: Killer whales breathe usually every 10 to 30 seconds for a series of a dozen or so short dives, followed by a dive lasting up to 4 minutes.

Mating and breeding: Breeding season is thought to last all year. Calves, about 2.4 m (8 ft), weighing 182 kg (400 lb), are born after a 13- to 16-month gestation period. Males reach sexual maturity at about 6.7 m (22 ft); females at about 5 m (16 ft). Calves are usually dependent on mothers for the first year.

Herding: Usually between 2 to 3 and 25 to 30, but herds of several thousand have been reported in Icelandic waters.

Distribution: All oceans; coastal waters and cooler regions preferred.

Migration: Some herds appear to move toward the equator during winter and toward polar regions during summer, but definitive migratory patterns are not known. Some herds are endemic to specific regions all year long.

Natural history notes: Killer whales are very active animals on the surface, often leaping clear of the water. Very inquisitive, they often approach small boats at close range.

A group of killer whales in the calm waters of Puget Sound, Washington. The very tall, straight dorsal fin of the animal on the right indicates a male.

IRRAWADDY DOLPHIN

lumbalumba

Family **Delphinidae**
Genus *Orcaella*
Species ***O. brevirostris*** (Gray, 1866)

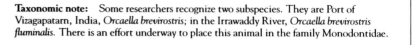

Taxonomic note: Some researchers recognize two subspecies. They are Port of Vizagapatarn, India, *Orcaella brevirostris*; in the Irrawaddy River, *Orcaella brevirostris fluminalis*. There is an effort underway to place this animal in the family Monodontidae.

The Irrawaddy dolphin inhabits fresh water as comfortably as coastal marine water. The animals travel upstream 10 miles or more and are well suited for river travel with their flexible bodies and necks and paddle-shaped flippers. Irrawaddy dolphins are slow-swimming animals that live exclusively in warm, tropical waters where they have been observed jumping clear of the water, as well as twisting and rolling while swimming on or near the surface.

Physical description: Body is long and somewhat stocky with a narrow peduncle region. The head is blunt. The rostrum consists merely of lips that appear mildly swollen. The blowhole is located slightly left of the forehead. The eyes are very well-developed. The neck is distinct and functional: The animal can turn its head without turning its body.

Color: Very dark gray, slightly lighter ventrally.

Fins and flukes: The small, rounded, slightly falcate dorsal fin is located well to the rear of the mid-back region, with a distinct ridge running from dorsal fin to flukes. Paddle-shaped flippers are slightly pointed at their tips. Narrow flukes are well spread and pointed at their tips.

Length and weight: Reaches 2.1 m (7 ft) and 100 kg (220 lb).

Teeth: 15 to 17 are located on each side of upper jaw, 12 to 14 slightly larger teeth on each side of lower jaw.

Feeding: Fish and crustaceans.

Breathing and diving: Dives average about a minute in duration. Occasionally the animals rise to make low, horizontal leaps from the surface. They have also been observed "spyhopping," in which just the head protrudes from the water.

Mating and breeding: Little is known. On July 4, 1979, the first baby was born in captivity in Djakarta. At birth it was 65 cm (25.5 in) long and weighed 5 kg (11 lb).

Herding: Groups of no more than 10 individuals.

Distribution: Coastal waters from the Bay of Bengal east to New Guinea and northern Australia; far up the Mekong, Irrawaddy, and Ganges Rivers.

Migration: No noticeable migration, but in certain regions of their distribution (Mekong River) their movements are dictated by the rising and falling of the rivers.

Natural history notes: These are very quiet animals. They have been observed swimming at speeds up to 20 to 25 kmph (15 to 18 mph).

Below, **the Irrawaddy dolphin is coastal and is comfortable in fresh as well as marine waters.**

Opposite, **with its blunt head, binocular vision and highly flexible neck, the Irrawaddy dolphin resembles the beluga whale.**

Stephen Leatherwood

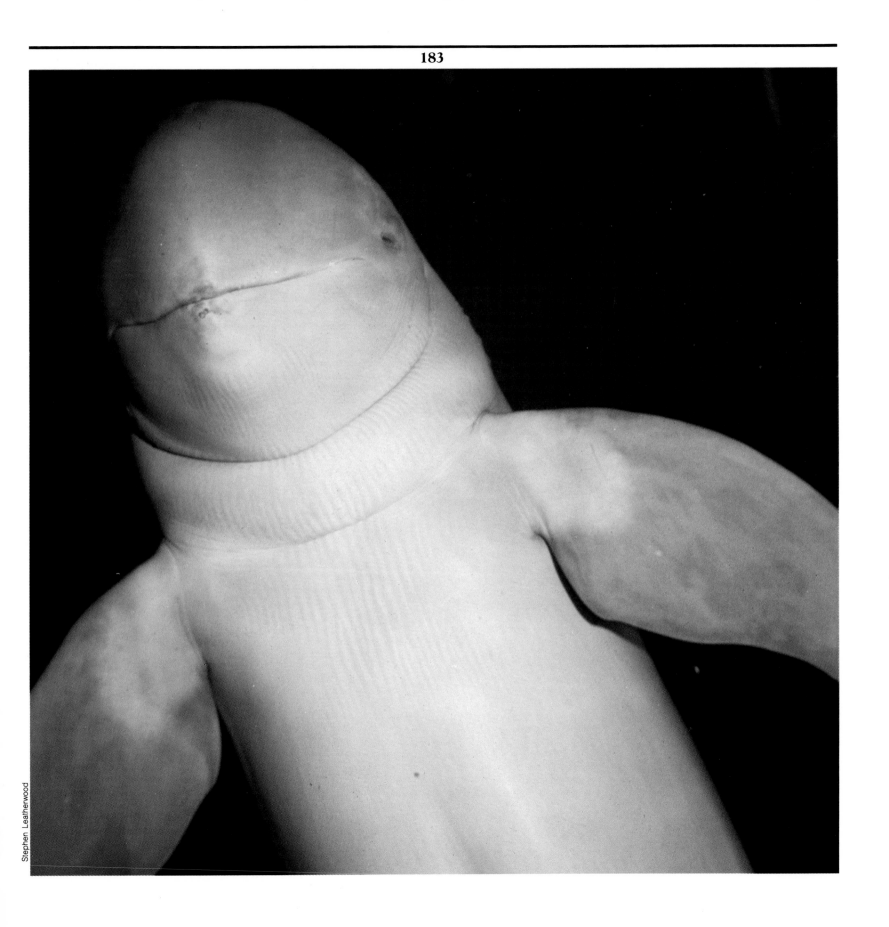

An Irrawaddy dolphin birth was captured in this remarkable set of photographs taken at the Jaya Ancol Oceanarium in Djakarta, Indonesia. As the mother swims in slow circles, the baby whale emerges tail first, its flukes and fetal folds visible. The newborn then heads immediately for its first breath at the surface, breaking its umbilical cord.

P. Arnantho

P. Arnantho

BELUGA AND NARWHAL
FAMILY: MONODONTIDAE

APPARENTLY, at some time in the evolution of dolphinlike creatures, some animals were trapped in an arctic environment by shifting patterns of ice and climate, and there they evolved successfully over the eons into the narwhal and beluga whales we know today. Both animals have retained freedom of movement in their neck vertebrae, lost their dorsal fins, developed thick layers of insulating blubber, and have adapted to spend their entire life cycles close to the advancing and retreating ice pack of the Northern Hemisphere. Both are gregarious animals, and both are oddities that have stirred the mythic imaginations of peoples over many centuries.

Medieval Europeans ascribed the long spiral tusk of the narwhal to the mythical beast they called a unicorn. Their tusks brought princely praise and reward to venturesome men who brought them back from the early voyages of northern exploration. Everywhere they were objects of curiosity. Today we know where the tusks originate, but they still pose questions: Of what use is the tusk to the narwhal? Why does it erupt through the gum only in males? And why only the left one of a pair? Why does it always spiral toward the left?

The beluga has no tusk, but its vociferous squeals and chirps, emmitted as it travels among the ice floes, often assembling in large herds to feed, have earned it the name "sea canary." People walking on the ice or drifting in a boat near a group of belugas hear a constant chorus of their canarylike songs.

Resembling a small beluga is the Irrawaddy dolphin (see page 182). Although the Irrawaddy dolphin is currently placed in the family Delphinidae, its anatomical similarities to the beluga have given rise to a movement to place it in the family Monodontidae with the beluga and narwhal despite its tropical distribution. ◄━━

Stephen Leatherwood

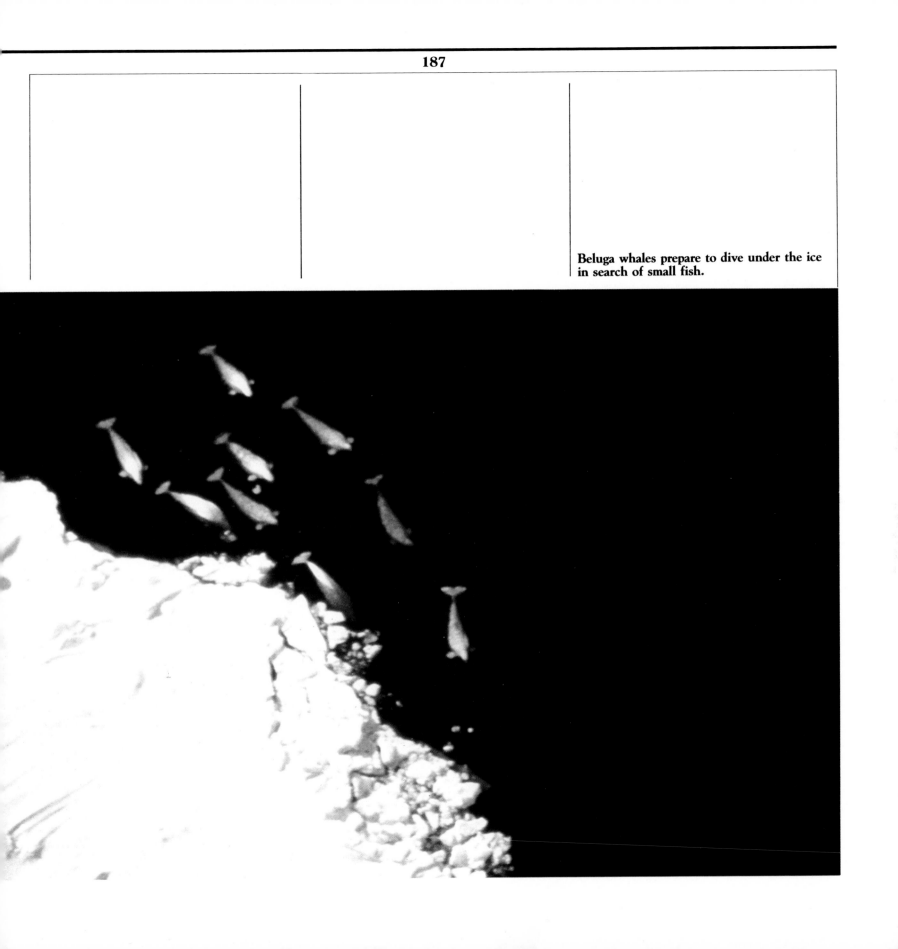

Beluga whales prepare to dive under the ice in search of small fish.

BELUGA

white whale   sea canary   belukha

Family **Monodontidae**
Genus *Delphinapterus*
Species *D. leucas*   (Pallas, 1776)

Belugas, like all other whales, are warm-blooded animals with a body temperature very close to that of humans, and yet belugas have survived and adapted quite successfully in their icy, Arctic habitat. This is made possible in part by their thick layer of fat, or blubber, which acts as a thermal regulator, preventing body heat from escaping. The beluga, like the right whale and the bowhead whale, has no dorsal fin, but rather a low dorsal ridge. A dorsal fin would seem to be a hindrance in a region where freeze over is a common occurrence.

The many high-pitched squeals and chirps emitted by the beluga can be heard through the hulls of boats, and are the basis for one of their secondary names, "sea canary." They are among the most vocal of all cetaceans.

Physical description: Extremely stocky, fat animal with disproportionately small head. The blowhole is set slightly to the left of the prominent forehead. It has a slight but discernible beak.

Color: Snow white overall. Young are brown with gray dorsal spots, turning gray and then white as they mature.

Fins and flukes: A narrow ridge notched laterally to form a series of very small bumps runs down the back in place of a dorsal fin. Short, wide flippers are often rounded at their tips. The broad flukes are very well-developed, pointed, and swept back at their tips, with a definite median notch.

Length and weight: Reach about 5 m (16 ft) and 1,100 kg (2,400 lb). Males grow slightly larger than females.

Teeth: 8 to 11 conical teeth are found in each side of the upper jaw, 8 to 9 in each side of the lower jaw.

Feeding: Feeds on a wide spectrum of shallow-water organisms, such as decapod crustaceans, cephalopods, and schooling fish.

Breathing and diving: They exhibit a variety of behavior, including slow and rapid motion while swimming, and more normal dolphinlike breathing when they rise to the surface, blow, drop out of sight for up to a minute, and rise to blow again.

Mating and breeding: Breeding season is June to August. Calves, 1.5 m (5 ft) are born after a 14-month gestation period, followed by a 20-month lactation. Males reach sexual maturity at about 9 years, females at about 5 years. Calving occurs at 3-year intervals.

Herding: Less than a dozen, often in single file. During southern migration small herds join to form large ones numbering several hundred animals.

Distribution: Arctic Ocean and adjacent seas. These whales frequent shallow waters and estuarine regions.

Migration: Southern migration in autumn from Arctic to Maritime Provinces for birthing and mating. They are regularly observed in the St. Lawrence and Saguenay rivers in late spring and summer. Sightings have occurred as far as 1,100 km (700 m) up the Yukon River and the St. Lawrence River to Quebec.

Natural history notes: Belugas are thought to live 35 to 50 years.

Nicknamed "sea canaries" for their high-pitched underwater sounds, beluga whales seem to be extremely intelligent.

Opposite, **born gray, beluga whales gradually turn white with age. They are the only truly white cetaceans.**

Kenneth C. Balcomb, III

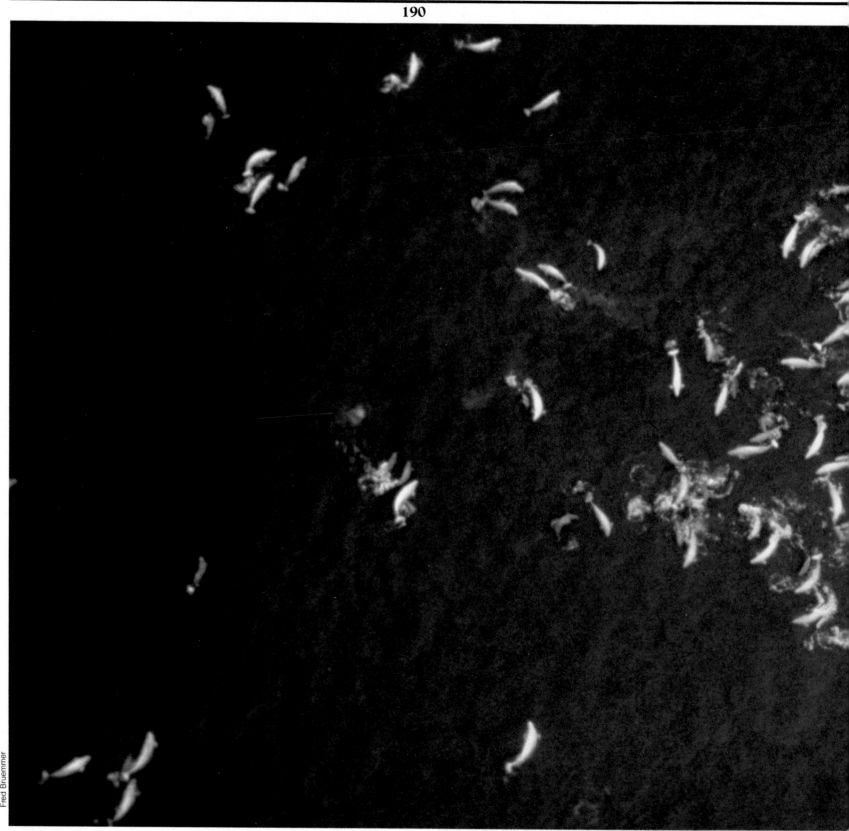

Gregarious belugas are observed often in groups of several thousand animals.

NARWHAL

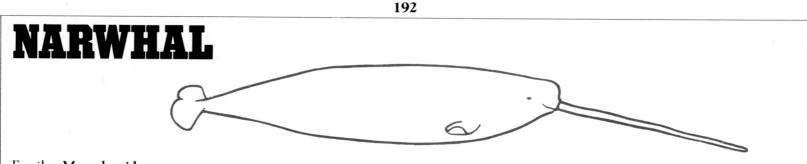

Family **Monodontidae**
Genus *Monodon*
Species ***M. monoceros***   Linnaeus, 1758

The narwhal is one of the two cetaceans which spend their entire lives in Arctic waters, the other being the bowhead whale. (The beluga migrates to warmer water to breed.) The narwhal is a very slow swimmer, seldom exceeding 6 kmph (4 mph). Large numbers of narwhals are trapped underwater occasionally by the rapid freezing of openings in the ice above them. Open breathing holes are of such great value that narwhals and walruses will fight for possession of them.

The most notable characteristic of the narwhal is its tusk, usually present only in adult males. The tusk is a living tooth which grows from the skull through the upper lip to a length of about 2.4 m (8 ft). It is one of two teeth in the upper jaw, although the second seldom erupts from the gum. Spiralling counterclockwise, the tusk contains living pulp. Although theories abound regarding the use or uses to which the narwhal puts its tusk, no one is sure of its function. It is doubtful that it is used to root out prey from the bottom sediments, for the tusk is usually covered with algae. It would seem to be an awkward weapon for combat, although on at least one occasion a male narwhal skull was found to have been penetrated by the tusk of another male.

Like the beluga (page 188), the narwhal is an Arctic dweller, inhabiting the circumpolar seas of the Northern Hemisphere. The two animals, however, occupy different niches as belugas frequent coastal waters and venture into rivers, while narwhals are deep-water animals.

Fred Bruemmer

Male narwhals cruise slowly through Arctic waters.

Illustrated by Larry A. Foster

Physical description: Its tusk is this animal's most obvious physical attribute. The body is somewhat stocky with a rounded, relatively small head.

Color: Varies with age from dark blue-gray in juveniles to brown-gray in adults. The dorsal region is covered with leopardlike spots.

Fins and flukes: A series of small bumps on the dorsal region replace a dorsal fin. Small, rounded flippers usually have upturned tips. Well-developed flukes are pointed at their tips with convex trailing edges. The young closely resemble young belugas.

Length and weight: Females reach 4 to 4.5 m (13 to 15 ft) and weigh 900 kg (2,000 lb). Males reach 4.7 m (15.5 ft) excluding tusk, and weigh about 1,600 kg (3,500 lb).

Teeth: Two in upper jaw only. In the adult male, the left tooth develops into the tusk, which may exceed 2.4 m (8 ft) in length. (In the female, the teeth seldom erupt through the gums.) The male's tusk spirals in a counterclockwise direction.

Feeding: Squid, Greenland halibut, polar cod, flounder, shrimp, rockfish, and crab.

Breathing and diving: These animals occasionally find themselves trapped under shrinking breathing holes in the ice, an extremely hazardous situation unless another breathing hole can be found quickly.

Mating and breeding: Conception probably occurs in mid-April. Calves, 1.5 m (5 ft) and about 80 kg (175 lb), are born after nearly 15 months' gestation. Births occur around mid-July. Females give birth at 3-year intervals.

Herding: Up to 2,000, in groups of between 10 and 20.

Distribution: High Arctic, mainly in deep water, and north polar seas.

Migration: Annual, with movement of the ice. They travel south as far as the coast of Labrador in fall, when ice forms; north to ice pack in spring.

Natural history notes: These animals often raise their heads above the water exposing the tusk.

A female and a tusked male narwhal are illustrated here. Found only on males, the tusk is a living tooth, spiraling from the skull through the upper lip and reaching a length of about 2.4 m (8 ft).

FRESHWATER DOLPHINS
FAMILY: PLATANISTIDAE

Ganges and Indus River dolphins   Amazon River dolphin   Chinese river dolphin   franciscana dolphin

DURING the great radiation, or dispersion, of marine mammals in the Miocene epoch, at least one group of cetaceans moved into estuarine and freshwater habitats, swimming far up the large rivers in tropical regions of the world. These animals were the platanistids, or freshwater dolphins, now represented by four genera found exclusively in South America and Asia.

All the freshwater dolphins retain certain skeletal characteristics that are relatively primitive by comparison with other cetaceans' structures, and they are similar to those of the ancestors of all small cetaceans. Freshwater dolphins have extremely long beaks (one-fifth to one-seventh of the overall body length) and interlocking conical teeth to grasp fish and invertebrates stirred up from river bottoms. Typically, they have poor eyesight; the turbid waters of their habitats make good vision unnecessary. They do possess excellent echolocation abilities and make social noises as well, indicating that they branched off from their marine cousins after those adaptations were well underway.

Because of their shy habits, the freshwater dolphins are surrounded by superstition and are generally little known. In spite of their proximity to the human populations that crowd the shores of the great rivers where they live, they have not generally been killed intentionally for food. Nonetheless, their numbers are dwindling in many areas, due to pollution, irrigation projects, and other human activities.

It has recently been proposed that the four genera of river dolphins represent four evolutionary departures from primitive dolphins and that each therefore deserves familial taxonomic status. While the evidence for this is compelling, we must wait until the arguments are aired in scientific literature. Here and elsewhere it is better to take the conservative approach in matters of classification. ➤

David K. Caldwell

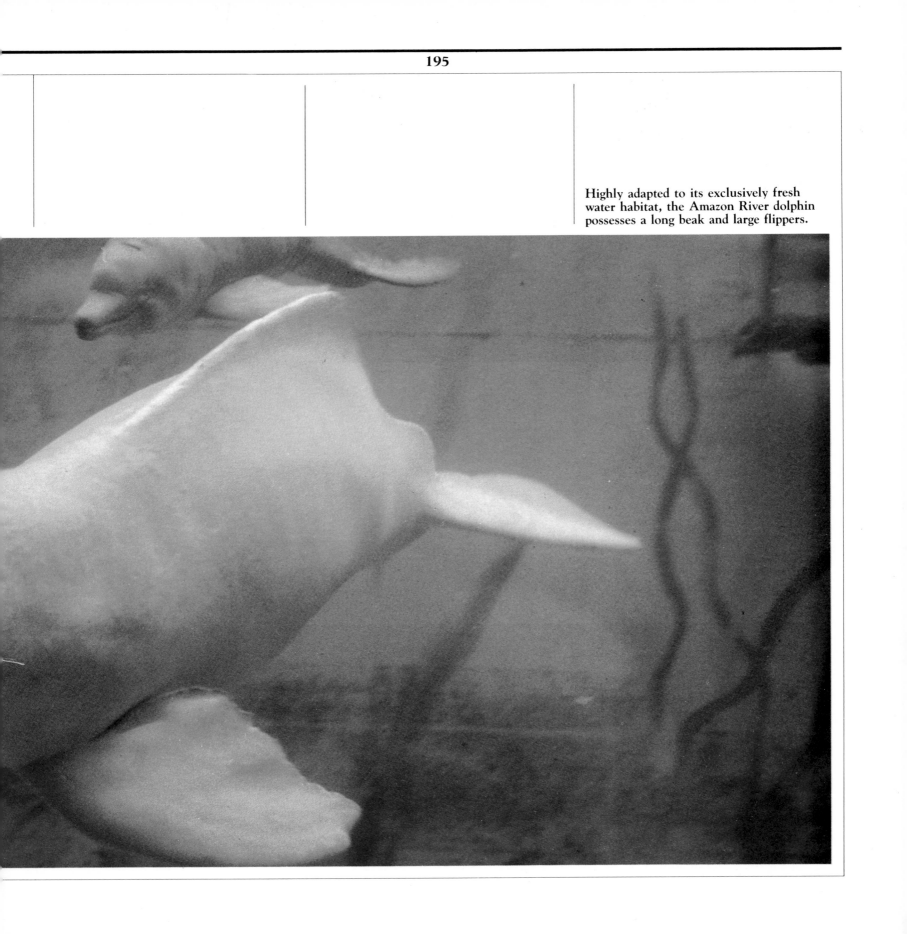

Highly adapted to its exclusively fresh water habitat, the Amazon River dolphin possesses a long beak and large flippers.

GANGES AND INDUS RIVER DOLPHINS

susu   side-swimming dolphin

Family   **Platanistidae**
Genus   *Platanista*
Species   ***P. gangetica***   (Ganges River Dolphin) (Roxburgh, 1801)
   P. minor   (Indus River Dolphin) Owen, 1853

Taxonomic note: Researchers occasionally use the previously accepted taxonomic labeling *Platanista indi,* although *Platanista minor* takes precedence.

The Ganges and Indus River dolphins are highly adapted to their environment. Other than distinguishing between dark and light, their degenerated eyesight plays an insignificant part in the animals' daily routine. Their bodies are extremely limber and their flippers broad and paddle-shaped in contrast to the more rigid, streamlined flippers of marine dolphins. The neck is flexible, the beak long, and the teeth needle sharp; presumably all these attributes help the dolphins to capture fish through ability, rather than sheer speed. They have excellent echolocation senses enabling them to navigate their home estuaries. Animals that have been kept captive in clear water appear to swim most frequently on their sides.

Although clearly separated geographically, the Ganges and Indus River dolphins are essentially the same.

Physical description: The rostrum is thin and long, averaging 18 cm (7 in), but always longer in the female. The blowhole consists of a single lateral slit to the left of the rear forehead.

Color: A dark gray dorsal region converges to lighter gray flanks and ventral regions.

Fins and flukes: The dorsal fin consists of a very small rise to the rear of the midback; it falls to follow the dorsal ridge to well-defined flukes. The flukes are pointed at their tips and have a slight median notch. The flippers are large and rounded on the leading edge.

Length and weight: They reach 1.8 to 2.4 m (6 to 8 ft) and 73 kg (160 lb).

Teeth: About 26 to 37 small, thin teeth appear in each side of the upper and lower jaws, increasing in size from back to front.

Feeding: Diet includes shrimp, catfish, carp, and gobies.

Breathing and diving: These dolphins breathe at 3- to 30-second intervals, often raising the head out of the water at an angle.

Mating and breeding: Calves are born at about 75 cm (28 in), possibly between April and July. The gestation period is believed to be 8 to 9 months. Weaning occurs within a year, although solid food can be taken after 2 months. Sexual maturity is attained at 1.7 m (5.5 ft) in males, and 1.7 to 2 m

California Academy of Sciences

Steinhart Aquarium

(5.5 to 6.5 ft) in females. It has been suggested that females bear calves at intervals of at least 2 years.

Herding: They swim alone or in groups of fewer than 12.

Distribution: Ganges River dolphins are found throughout most of the Ganges, Brahmaputra, and Karnaphuli rivers of India and Bangladesh. The Indus River dolphin is found in the Indus River of Pakistan.

Migration: During summer, Ganges River dolphins travel down the Hoogly River to Calcutta and down the Pusser River to Chalna.

Natural history notes: These animals have extremely sensitive regions along the leading margin of the flippers that apparently are used (along with the long beak) to probe the bottom mud for food, resulting in their nickname of side-swimming dolphin.

Above, almost blind, the Indus and Ganges River dolphins can discern shadows visually, but orient themselves primarily by an excellent echolocation system.

Opposite, this Indus River dolphin swims sideways, enabling the extremely sensitive edges of its flippers to comb the mud for food fish.

AMAZON RIVER DOLPHIN

bouto

Family **Platanistidae**
Genus ***Inia***
Species ***I. geoffrensis*** (de Blainville, 1817)

Taxonomic note: Contemporary research indicates the presence of three distinct populations which may warrant classification as subspecies: northern population, *Inia geoffrensis humboltiana*; central population, *Inia geoffrensis geoffrensis*; southern population, *Inia geoffrensis*. Physical differences among populations include different tooth counts, and all three populations are separated geographically by mountain ranges.

The largest freshwater dolphins, the Amazon River dolphins developed unusual features—as have many other animals inhabiting the Amazon River system. As might be expected of a species inhabiting turbid waters, these dolphins' eyes are small; however, the animals have keen eyesight. As with all exclusively freshwater dolphins, the beak is unusually long, yet stout; the flippers are very broad rather than streamlined and are flexible at the axila (armpit). Although the animals reach 2.7 m (9 ft) in length, they are able to maneuver well in close quarters.

Amazon River dolphins spend a great deal of time in physical contact with one another. They have been observed heaving their bodies out of the water onto mud banks for food, rolling and twisting to return to the water. Amazon tribesmen believe that killing this animal brings very bad luck.

Physical Description: Most dolphins are born with hairs on the beak, many of which disappear early in life. The presence of those hairs that remain is unique among dolphins; apparently they are used while the animal probes the mud for food. The body is large and soft, forming folds when the head is moved. The bulbous forehead is small in proportion to the body. The blowhole is a rectangular slit.

Color: Some animals are pink overall; others are gray dorsally, converging to pink ventrally. The many color variations suggest that color is subject to environmental conditions.

Fins and flukes: The dorsal area rises from both the posterior and anterior ridges to meet at a point just to the rear of the midback region. Here there is a single pointed rise where a dorsal fin would be on most other dolphins. The flippers are very large and well spread. The flukes, often serrated on the trailing edge, are very large and well spread also, with a median notch. The tips are nearly pointed.

Length and weight: They reach 2.5 to 3 m (8.25 to 9.75 ft) and nearly 90 kg (200 lb). Males are slightly larger than females.

Teeth: There are 24 to 30 large, conical teeth on each side of the upper and lower jaws, although the tooth count varies among geographic populations.

Feeding: They feed on turtles, catfish and other freshwater fish, and crustaceans.

David K. Caldwell

Breathing and diving: The Amazon River dolphin breathes every 35 to 40 seconds, with a maximum recorded dive of 112 seconds. Its blow is very noisy and very high, up to 1.8 m (6 ft).

Mating and breeding: Infants are born between July and September, about 75 cm (30 in) long and weighing just over 1 kg (2.2 lb), after a gestation period believed to be from 9 to 12 months. Sexual maturity in males is reached at about 2 m (7 ft), and in females at 1.7 m (5.5 ft), at an unknown age.

Herding: Observed individually or in groups of up to 3; rarely up to 20 individuals.

David K. Caldwell

Distribution: Amazon River dolphins are found in all main rivers in the Orinoco and Amazon river systems. The northern population inhabits the Orinoco, Atabapo, and Temi rivers and their tributaries. The central population ranges throughout the Amazon basin and the rivers of Peru and Brazil. The southern population, sometimes called the Bolivian dolphin, also inhabits the Amazon basin and the rivers of Peru.

Migration: No information is available.

Natural history notes: Ordinarily a very slow moving animal, the Amazon River dolphin may swim rapidly to breathe or feed, swimming to just below the surface, where it breaks in a horizontal position.

Above, a group of Amazon River dolphins maintain physical contact as they swim in their tank at Marineland of Florida. Commonplace in the wild, this contact is probably a result of the murky river habitat.

Opposite, the Amazon River dolphin, the largest of all freshwater dolphins, is found in many river systems throughout Brazil, Bolivia, and Argentina.

CHINESE RIVER DOLPHIN

whitefin dolphin
white-flag dolphin
white dolphin

Family **Platanistidae**
Genus *Lipotes*
Species *L. vexillifer*   Miller, 1918

Because the Chinese river dolphin is indigenous to the waters within the People's Republic of China, western researchers have had little access to it or information concerning its habits and natural history. In January 1980, Chinese researchers from the Institute of Hydrobiology in Wuhan captured and are now maintaining a Chinese river dolphin, the first of its species in captivity. Much of the information contained in this chapter comes from the information provided by the researchers studying these rare and endangered animals in the wild as well as the specimen in captivity.

Hunting Chinese river dolphins is forbidden, but many of the animals are accidently killed when they feed on fish caught by fishermen using hooks on long lines. These animals become highly agitated prior to storms, and because of this they have developed a reputation over many hundreds of years as bearers of omens.

Illustrated by Larry A. Foster

Left, the rare Chinese river dolphin, illustrated here, is frequently killed when it feeds on fish caught by fisherman using hooks on long lines.

Opposite, this young Chinese river dolphin was captured in Wuhan, China, for research. These animals are often trapped by accident in fishing nets and killed.

Physical description: Like the Amazon River dolphin, the Chinese river dolphin is stocky with a long, thin, flattened rostrum, bowed slightly upward. The blowhole is slightly to the left of the center of the forehead. This animal develops a thick fat layer during winter.

Color: Gray or bluish-gray dorsal region blends to white ventrally.

Fins and flukes: The dorsal fin is a triangular rise in the midback region. Flippers are small, wide, and rounded at their tips. Flukes are well-developed, pointed at their tips, with a small median notch.

Length and weight: It reaches 2.1 to 2.4 m (7 to 8 ft) and 82 kg (180 lb); females are slightly larger.

Teeth: About 31 to 36 per side are found in each of the upper and lower jaws. The fact that the teeth are wrinkled was previously thought to indicate that food is crushed prior to ingestion. Recent observations confirm that food is swallowed whole and uncrushed.

Feeding: Feed on eel-like, scaly catfish, caught near the bottom.

Breathing and diving: While swimming they breathe every 5 to 30 seconds; the longest timed dive is one minute.

Mating and breeding: Fully developed fetuses have been found measuring 57 cm (22.5 in) in length and weighing slightly over 4.5 kg (10 lb). Gestation period is 6 months, very short for dolphins.

Herding: Almost always found in pairs, but groups of up to 10 have been sighted.

Distribution: Chinese river dolphins are found almost exclusively in middle and lower regions of the Yangtze and Quintangjiang rivers. These very shy animals are the survivors of heavy incidental killings. They move about within their distribution, depending on their needs, to areas suitable for feeding, or for mating and breeding. They are very often found near sand banks.

Migration: No information is available.

Natural history notes: Chinese river dolphins possess a highly developed echolocation faculty. These highly intelligent and gregarious animals are thought to live about 30 years.

FRANCISCANA DOLPHIN

La Plata River dolphin

Family **Platanistidae**
Genus *Pontoporia*
Species *P. blainvillei*   (Gervais and d'Orbigny, 1844)

Illustrated by Larry A. Foster

The only member of the freshwater dolphin family to be found in marine waters, the franciscana dolphin may be found in fresh, brackish, or salt water, but not in rivers. It is an obscure animal that inhabits isolated areas, and little is known of its habits and natural history.

Physical Description: Somewhat stocky body with disproportionately small head and long, thin beak—the longest beak-to-body ratio of any dolphin. Juveniles are much stockier with a distinctly shorter beak.

Color: Pale brown dorsally converging to lighter brown ventrally. Some animals—known to fishermen as "white ghosts" and observed in the La Plata River estuary—are nearly all white.

Fins and flukes: The distinct triangular dorsal fin is located on the midback region where it extends back as a ridge to the flukes. The flippers are paddle-shaped and rounded at their tips. Well-spread flukes are pointed at their tips, with a discernible median notch.

Length and weight: For males, 1.5 m (5 ft) and 32 kg (70 lb); for females, 1.7 m (5.5 ft) and 40 kg (90 lb).

Teeth: 50 or more sharp, toothpick-shaped teeth are found in each row of upper and lower jaws.

Feeding: At least 19 species of fish, 3 species of shrimp, and 1 species of squid. They are predominently bottom feeders.

Breathing and diving: No information is available.

Mating and breeding: Calves are about 70 cm (27 in) long, 7 to 9 kg (15 to 20 lb) in weight. They are believed to be born from October to January. Gestation is 10.5 months; lactation lasts 9 months. Sexual maturity occurs at age 2 or 3, when males are 1.3 m (4.5 ft) and females 1.4 m (4.6 ft). Calving interval is typically every 2 years.

Herding: Numerous observations suggest they do not herd but swim alone or in groups up to five.

Distribution: Apparently shallow waters only, in the coastal Atlantic Ocean from the Valdes Peninsula and La Plata River delta of Argentina to the Tropic of Capricorn near Rio de Janeiro, Brazil.

Migration: Rarely observed in the La Plata River delta during winter, which suggests migration at this time, northward along the coast.

Natural history notes: These animals are believed to live between 15 and 20 years.

The franciscana dolphin, illustrated here, is known to fishermen as the "white ghost" since its body is nearly all white.

PORPOISES
FAMILY: PHOCOENIDAE

harbor porpoise

Gulf of California harbor porpoise

spectacled porpoise

Burmeister's porpoise

finless porpoise

Dall's porpoise

ERHAPS the most common question asked by persons who become acquainted with cetaceans is "What's the difference between a dolphin and a porpoise?"

The issue is muddled because the two names have been used interchangeably by laymen, fishermen, and scientists alike for as long as the words have been spoken. Strictly speaking, the word *dolphin* is properly applied to the smaller species within the family Delphinidae and the word *porpoise* to those within the family Phocoenidae, but that just diverts the reader to family names and does not explain the difference. For those who have the opportunity to look in their mouths, dolphins have cone-shaped teeth, and porpoises have little spade-shaped teeth. There are also differences in the form of the skull bones and other features, but these are even less useful field characters that require dissection to demonstrate. The simplest way to distinguish between dolphins and porpoises is to try to remember the features of the porpoise species that are likely to be in the area of observation (in any given area there normally will not be more than two). Everything else one might see is at least not a porpoise. In the tropics, the chances are that you will not see a porpoise, unless it is the finless porpoise of coastal India, Asia, and Japan, or the harbor porpoise near the Cape Verde Islands off West Africa.

One porpoise species, *Phocoenoides dalli,* occurs only in the North Pacific ocean, and another species, *Phocoena phocoena,* the most specialized member of its genus, occurs coastally and discontinuously only in the Northern Hemisphere. Two other species, *Phocoena dioptrica* and *Phocoena spinipinnis,* are found only in the Southern Hemisphere, mostly around coastal South America. One of the latter species apparently gave rise during the late Pleistocene to *P. sinus* which occurs only in the Gulf of California.

As a group, the porpoises seem to have trouble with en-tanglement and drowning in fishing nets of various types which were not set for them. It may be that this is due to an inability to acoustically "see" the nets with their echolocation sounds, or it may be due to the preponderantly coastal distribution of both nets and porpoises. Another problem that the phocoenids are having in their coastal environments in regions of high industralization concerns the accumulation of pollutants in their tissues. While the effects of these pollutants on body functions and survival is not yet known, levels of some contaminants are extraordinarily high, and there is cause for concern.

John Dziadecki

Above, a dramatic photograph of a harbor porpoise (foreground) and a bottlenose dolphin reveals differences in beak and melon.

Opposite, in the wild, mother finless porpoises sometimes carry their young on their backs.

HARBOR PORPOISE

common porpoise

Family **Phocoenidae**
Genus *Phocoena*
Species *P. phocoena*   (Linnaeus, 1758)

Taxonomic note: Those harbor porpoises found in the Black Sea are occasionally given a separate classification of *Phocoena phocoena relicta*, an alleged subspecies. Another taxonomic name seldom used today but synonymous with *Phocoena phocoena* is *Phocoena vomerina*.

As its alternative common name suggests, *Phocoena phocoena* is the most commonly seen of all porpoises. It swims at a maximum speed of about 13 kmph (8 mph) and will occasionally leap entirely clear of the water when breathing. It does not approach ships, nor does it ride their bow-waves, although it has been known to approach small inflatable boats.

Physical description: Stocky body.

Color: Brown or dark gray dorsally, converging to a lighter gray at the flanks, often distinguished by a well-defined color change beginning just behind the forehead, running along the flanks, and ending at the tail stock. Flippers and flukes are dark with the flipper color extending from their leading margins to the corners of the mouth.

Fins and flukes: The triangular dorsal fin is located on the midback region. Flippers are small, well rounded at tips and along the leading edges. Small, thin flukes are extremely well-defined, and rounded at their tips, with a definite median notch.

Length and weight: They reach 1.8 m (6 ft) and about 90 kg (200 lb). Females are slightly larger than males.

Teeth: 23 to 28 small, spade-shaped teeth are found on each side of the upper jaw, 22 to 26 on each side of the lower jaw.

Feeding: Herring, cod, sole, squid, and crustaceans.

Breathing and diving: Harbor porpoises breathe about every 15 seconds and do not stay submerged for more than 3 or 4 minutes.

Mating and breeding: Mating is generally believed to occur from March to July. A 76 cm (30 in), 6.4 to 10 kg (14 to 22 lb) calf is born after a gestation period of 8 to 10 months. Sexual maturity is reached at 4 years. Females can give birth at 24-month intervals.

Herding: Usually they are seen in a pair or groups, 5 to 10 in each; they may travel in herds up to 100.

Distribution: Coastal waters of the North Atlantic from Delaware and Senegal north to the Davis Strait, Iceland, and the White Sea; coastal waters of the North Pacific from Japan and Baja California to Point Barrow, Alaska.

Migration: To the northernmost part of their Atlantic distribution during summer, the southern part of their distribution in winter.

GULF OF CALIFORNIA HARBOR PORPOISE

vaquita
cochito

Family **Phocoenidae**
Genus ***Phocoena***
Species ***P. sinus***   Norris and McFarland, 1958

The first confirmation of this animal's existence occurred in 1950 when Kenneth S. Norris discovered a single skeleton on a beach in eastern Baja California. Since that time the Gulf of California harbor porpoise, the smallest of its genus, has been sighted occasionally, although very little has been learned about it. It is an extremely timid creature in the wild and tries to avoid being sighted, evidently with some success, since to this date there are no known photographs of it alive and few specimens have been studied by researchers. The animal is thought by some Mexican fishermen to be a *deunde*, a creature inhabited by a supernatural spirit. It has the most restricted distribution of any cetacean.

Physical description: Mexican shrimp fishermen have reported and described several specimens taken accidently in their nets: There is no beak, and the blowhole is situated well to the left on the forehead.

Color: Lead-gray above, gradually lightening to white below; no discernible black line along eye-to-eye crease.

Fins and flukes: The dorsal fin is reported to be much more prominent than that of the harbor porpoise (page 206); one animal possessed a dorsal fin that was extremely tall and slightly falcate. Flippers are small, round at the tips and on the leading edges. The thin flukes are small well-developed, nearly pointed at the tips, with a definite median notch.

Length and weight: Reaches at least 1.4 m (4.5 ft).

Teeth: The upper jaw of the specimen contained 41 small, spade-shaped teeth, the lower jaw 36 teeth.

Feeding: Remains of small fish (grunts and gulf croakers) were found in the stomach of one porpoise.

Breathing and diving: Observed animals usually rise to the surface very quickly, blow unobtrusively, and dive without raising flukes, disappearing for long periods of time.

Mating and breeding: Mexican fishermen report May and June sightings of adults with young estimated at 60 cm (24 in) in the estuary of the Rio Colorado at the head of the Gulf.

Herding: On most sightings two animals have been observed together.

Distribution: Found only in the upper Gulf of California.

Natural history notes: They pursue an erratic course after diving and surface in unpredictable locations.

Opposite, these harbor porpoises pause on
the surface off the Gulf of Farallones, near
San Francisco, California.

Above, an extraordinary photograph of a
harbor porpoise that swam by a small
research boat in the St. Lawrence estuary.
Note its blunt head and triangular fin.

SPECTACLED PORPOISE

Family **Phocoenidae**
Genus *Phocoena*
Species *P. dioptrica*   Lahille, 1912

O f the four species of the genus *Phocoena*, two live in the southern hemisphere; the spectacled porpoise is one of them. It is known from only 10 specimens and is the largest of the four in the genus. Its color pattern is distinctive, especially the black circles around the eyes, which give the animal its common name.

Found only in the Southern Hemisphere, the spectacled porpoise, depicted here in a painting, is named for the black circles around the eyes.

Illustrated by Larry A. Foster

Physical description: Somewhat stocky. The head is small and rounded with no beak. The anus is located relatively near the flukes.

Color: Ventral white extends partially up the flanks to meet well-defined black covering the dorsal regions. The white also reaches above the eyes and terminates above the upper lip. Black lightens from the rear peduncle region to the tail stock, then darkens again, covering the dorsal side of the flukes. Eyes are encircled with black and lips are rimmed with black.

Fins and flukes: Flippers are small and rounded at their tips; the dorsal fin is longer along its leading margin, rounded at top, with no falcation, and is located slightly to the rear of the midback region. Flukes are small, nearly pointed at their tips, with a definite median notch.

Length and weight: Spectacled porpoises average 2 m (6.75 ft) for the male and 1.80 m (6 ft) for females, and an estimated 55 kg (120 lb).

Teeth: 21 small, spade-shaped teeth are found in each side of the upper jaw and 17 in each side of the lower jaw.

Feeding: No information is available.

Breathing and diving: No information is available.

Mating and breeding: One fetus, recorded July 1912, measured 46 cm (1.5 ft) long.

Herding: No information is available.

Distribution: Coast of Argentina and Uruguay, the Falkland Islands, and South Georgia.

Migration: No information is available.

Natural history notes: This is the largest of the *Phocoenas*. It is the only species in its genus to live near offshore islands as a permanent resident.

BURMEISTER'S PORPOISE

Family **Phocoenidae**
Genus *Phocoena*
Species *P. spinipinnis*   Burmeister, 1865

Burmeister's porpoise is one of two members of the genus *Phocoena* that live in the Southern Hemisphere, the other being the spectacled porpoise (page 210). Burmeister's porpoise is considered to be the most abundant coastal small cetacean in South American waters, and is thought to be distributed in both the Atlantic and Pacific oceans. Its most striking feature is the shape and position of the dorsal fin, which is triangular but very low and pointed to the rear so that it appears as a continuation of a dorsal ridge.

Illustrated by Larry A. Foster

Physical description: The body is stocky with a slight indentation at the blowhole. A sharp, well-defined ridge extends from the rear of the dorsal fin to the flukes.

Color: Almost completely dark, with a nearly white genital region, and some white on the chin from the tip of the lower jaw, spreading to and dissolving at the anterior ridges of the flippers.

Fins and flukes: The dorsal fin begins well to the rear of the midback region and follows the dorsal ridge out until it curves down and in toward the body to resemble a triangular fin slanted sharply to the rear. About half a dozen small tubercles are located on the leading edge of the dorsal fin. Flippers are paddle-shaped and rounded at their tips. Flukes are very well-developed, slightly rounded at their tips, with a definite median notch.

Length and weight: This porpoise reaches at least 1.9 m (6.25 ft) and an estimated 68 to 73 kg (150 to 160 lb).

Teeth: There are 14 to 16 teeth in each upper jaw; 17 to 19 in each lower jaw.

Feeding: Known to feed on squid.

Breathing and diving: No information is available.

Mating and breeding: A 46 cm (1.5 ft) fetus was collected in Uruguayan waters in late February or early March.

Herding: In most sightings so far, about a dozen or fewer animals appeared together.

Distribution: Shallow waters of both coasts of South America—east coast of South America from Uruguay to Patagonia, Argentina; west coast from Paita, Peru, to Valdivia, Chile. Apparently these are two distinct stocks, one in the Atlantic, one in the Pacific.

Migration: No information is available.

The most common cetacean in South American waters, the Burmeister's porpoise, seen here in a painting, has a unique triangular dorsal fin pointing to the rear.

FINLESS PORPOISE

Family **Phocoenidae**
Genus *Neophocaena*
Species *N. phocaenoides*   (G. Cuvier, 1829)

White and black variations have been observed among finless porpoises. Although these may represent separate subspecies, insufficient evidence has been gathered to confirm or deny this. The finless porpoise is the only true porpoise with no dorsal fin, although a low ridge runs down the back. This animal lives in both fresh and salt water and will ascend considerable distances up rivers. It possesses many of the same traits as the Irrawaddy dolphin (page 182), with its riverine habits, flexible neck, and paddle-shaped flippers. It very much resembles a small beluga (page 188).

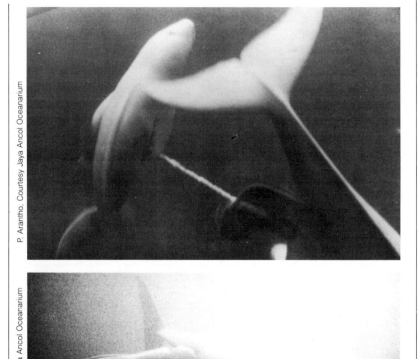

P. Arantho, Courtesy Jaya Ancol Oceanarium

Physical description: Head rounded in contour with slightly stocky body. A prominently rounded dorsal ridge stretches from the midback region to the tail stock. Many are reported to have pink eyes.

Color: Pale gray with a blue tinge on the back and sides. Off-white on the ventral regions, particularly the head and anterior regions of the rump.

Fins and flukes: There is no dorsal fin. The flippers are long, broad, and pointed at their tips. Long, thin flukes are rounded at their tips, with a definite median notch.

Length and weight: Reaches a length of 1.4 to 1.8 m (4.5 to 6 ft) and about 45 kg (100 lb).

Teeth: 15 to 19 short, compressed, spade-shaped teeth are found on each side of the upper and lower jaws.

Feeding: Small fish, prawns, cuttlefish, and squid.

Breathing and diving: Prior to a dive, which lasts from 45 to 75 seconds, they breathe 3 to 4 times in quick succession every 7 to 13 seconds.

Mating and breeding: It has been suggested that calves are born in August at 7 to 9 kg (15 to 20 lb).

Herding: Up to 50 have been observed, subdivided into groups of about 5.

Right, **the birth of a finless porpoise. Born tail first, the calf leaves its mother immediately, and heads for the surface, breaking its umbilical cord and taking its first breath.**

Distribution: Warm coastal waters and certain rivers from Pakistan east to Korea, Japan, Borneo, and Java.

Migration: No information is available.

Natural history notes: Ordinarily these animals swim just below the surface with rapid, erratic movements. Mothers have been observed swimming with calves on their back's; the calf comes all the way out of the water on the mother's back when she rises to the surface. The calf may use a rough skin patch on the mother's dorsal region to secure itself for a free ride.

Left, a finless porpoise swims in Toba Aquarium, Japan. Note its flexible neck.

Below, a finless porpoise swims with her calf in Toba Aquarium, Japan. Note the small, rounded ridge running along the mother's back.

W.J. Houck

Masami Furuta

DALL'S PORPOISE

Family **Phocoenidae**
Genus *Phocoenoides*
Species *P. dalli* (True, 1885)

Taxonomic note: Animals with variable white flank coloration and which allegedly possess a greater number of teeth still are referred to occasionally as *Phocoenoides truii,* or True's porpoise. Recent observational research, however, confirms a vast and diverse mixture of color patterns within individual herds, seriously weakening the evidence for existence of a second species or subspecies.

Extremely chunky animals with tiny heads and very small flukes and flippers, Dall's porpoises sometimes cut through the water at tremendous speeds, sending up characteristic "rooster tails" behind and thin sheets of water over their backs. Dall's porpoises are avid bow-wave riders and sometimes will travel hundreds of yards for a free ride at the front of a ship. At other times, particularly when feeding, they seem uninterested in ships.

Physical description: These animals have very stocky bodies with small appendages. A slight forehead indentation is present at the blowhole, and a large hump present on the dorsal ridge between the dorsal fin and the flukes.

Color: They are jet black, with white from the anus to the midbelly and on the outer ridges of the flukes and dorsal fin, although many variations exist. Normally, the flanks are white from the head to the midpeduncle region, but nearly all-white and all-black animals have been observed.

Fins and flukes: The dorsal fin is triangular, prominent, and pointed, located at the midback. The flippers are very small and rounded at the tips. The small flukes are nearly pointed at the tips with a slight median notch.

Length and weight: They reach a length of 2.1 m (6.75 ft) and about 145 kg (320 lb).

Teeth: They possess about 19 to 23 small, spade-shaped teeth in each side of the upper jaw, and about 20 to 24 in each of the lower jaw.

Feeding: Their known diet consists of lantern fish, squid, and schooling fish.

Mating and breeding: Calves of 100 cm (40 in) are born in late July and early August. The gestation period lasts about a year.

Right, **Dall's porpoises are avid bow-wave riders and very fast swimmers.**

Opposite, **taken from a ship's underwater observation port, this photograph reveals the extremely powerful body and striking coloration of the Dall's porpoise.**

Robert Pitman

Herding: They are found in groups numbering about one dozen.

Distribution: They are found in the immediate offshore waters of the North Pacific Ocean from Japan and southern California as far north as the Bering Sea.

Migration: They travel to the northern end of their range during the summer, southern end in the winter.

Robert Pitman

Gray whales swim along the California coast.

GLOSSARY

Anterior. Situated at or near the head.

Baleen (bə lēn′). A horny substance attached along the upper jaw forming a fringelike sieve enabling whales of the suborder Mysticeti to collect and retain food. Also known as whalebone.

Benthic. Of or living at the bottom of the ocean.

Blow. Moisture-laden air ejected from the lungs through the blowhole.

Bow-wave riding. Riding in the wave on either side of the bow of a moving ship using the vessel's speed to enhance the animal's own.

Breach. To leap from the water and land in the water again.

Bubble netting. Method of feeding in which the whale releases a series of bubbles from below a school of fish at the same time spiraling upward, concentrating the fish into one large mouthful.

Callosities. Natural yellowish or white horny growths that serve as a home for whale lice and barnacles.

Caudal fin. The tail fin of a marine vertebrate.

Conspecific. Of the same species.

Cookie-cutter shark. Small shark *Isistius brasiliensis* about 45 centimeters (18 inches) long, believed to cause scoop-shaped injuries in the skin of a number of species of large whales.

Copepod. Minute, shrimplike crustaceans.

Deep Scattering Layer (DSL). Stratified groups of organisms in ocean waters that scatter sound. Usually found during the day at depths of 200 to 800 meters (650 to 2600 feet).

Dorsal. On or near the back; on a whale, the upper surface.

Dorsal fin. The back fin.

Echolocation. The process in which whales send out and interpret sonarlike sound waves into information about their environment and location of prey.

Euphausid. An order of shrimplike crustaceans.

Falcate. Curved and tapering, sickle-shaped.

Flippers. Forelimbs of a marine mammal.

Flukes. Horizontal tail fin.

Grubbing. Method of feeding on organisms in which the whale stirs up the bottom sediment by pushing water out of its mouth, drawing in the material, sluicing the mouth with clean water, and swallowing the catch.

Herd. A homogeneous unit of animals of the same species.

Krill. Widely used Norwegian term for euphausids, shrimplike crustaceans up to 5 centimeters (2 inches) in length.

Lunge feeding. A method of feeding in which the whale swims rapidly around a school of fish, forcing it into a tight mass, and then takes them in one lunging gulp.

Logging. The act of lying still on or near the surface.

Median notch. The V-shaped cut on the posterior edge of the flukes.

Melon. Bulbous forehead of some cetaceans; it may be used in sound production.

Peduncle. Tail stock between the anus and the flukes.

Pelagic. Of or living in the open ocean.

Plankton. Generally microscopic organisms that drift or swim weakly in the upper levels of the ocean.

Pod. A small, genetically related family unit.

Posterior. Situated at or near the tail end.

Rorqual (rork′wəl). Baleen whales of the genus *Balaenoptera* having pleated throat grooves.

Rostrum. A whale's beak or snout.

Spermaceti. An organ located in the forehead of some cetaceans containing a high quality oil that may play a vital role in echolocation and may serve as a neutral buoyancy device.

Spyhopping. The act of raising the head vertically above the water, possibly to look around, investigate a disturbance, or navigate by coastline.

Stranding. As yet unexplained behavior in which whales beach themselves in shallow water and die.

Tail stock. See peduncle.

Throat pleats. Longitudinal grooves on the throat that expand allowing great quantities of sea water to be engulfed and filtered through baleen plates.

Ventral. Situated on or near the belly, on the lower surface of a whale.

Whale lice. Small crablike crustaceans that parasitize some species of whales.

SELECTED READINGS

ALLEN, K. RADWAY. *Conservation and Management of Whales.* Washington Sea Grant Publication, 1980.

BERNARD, K.H. *A Guide Book to South African Whales and Dolphins.* South African Museum, Guide No. 4, 1954.

BRUYNS, MORZER. *Field Guide to Whales and Dolphins.* Amsterdam, Netherlands: Uitgevery tor/n. v. Utgerery V. H. C. A. mees Zeiseniskade 14 II, 1971.

COFFEY, D.J. *Dolphins, Whales and Porpoises: An Encyclopedia of Marine Mammals.* New York: Collier Books, 1977.

COOK, JOSEPH J., and WILLIAM L. WISNER. *Blue Whales, Vanishing Leviathan.* New York: Dodd, Mead & Co., 1973.

DAUGHERTY, ANITA. *Marine Mammals of California.* Sacramento, California: California Department of Fish and Game, 1965.

Friends of the Earth. *The Whale Manual.* San Francisco, California: Friends of the Earth, 1978.

KATONA, STEVEN, DAVID RICHARDSON, and ROBIN HAZARD. *A Field Guide to the Whales and Seals of the Gulf of Maine.* 2d ed. Bar Harbor, Maine: College of the Atlantic, 1977.

LEATHERWOOD, STEPHEN, RANDALL R. REEVES, and LARRY FOSTER. *The Sierra Club Handbook of Whales and Dolphins.* San Francisco, California: Sierra Club Books, 1983.

MATTHEWS, L. HARRISON. *The Natural History of Whales.* New York: Columbia University Press, 1978.

McINTYRE, JOAN. *Mind in the Water.* New York: Charles Scribner's Sons, 1974.

NORRIS, KENNETH S. *Porpoise Watcher.* New York: W.W. Norton & Co., Inc., 1974.

——, ed. *Whales, Dolphins and Porpoises.* Berkeley, California: University of California Press, 1966.

ORR, ROBERT. *Marine Mammals of California.* Berkeley, California: University of California Press, 1972.

PRYOR, KAREN. *Lads Before the Wind.* New York: Harper & Row, 1975.

RIDGEWAY, SAM H., ed. *Mammals of the Sea.* Springfield, Illinois: Charles C. Thomas Publishers, 1972.

ROBSON, FRANK. *Thinking Dolphins, Talking Whales.* Wellington: A.H. & A.W. Reed, Ltd., 1976.

SCAMMON, CHARLES M. *Marine Mammals of the Northwestern Coast of North America, Together with an Account of the American Whale Fishery.* rev. ed. New York: Dover Publications, 1968.

SCHEVILL, WILLIAM E., ed. *The Whale Problem: A Status Report.* Cambridge, Massachusetts: Harvard University Press, 1974.

SLIJPER, E.J. *Whales.* London: Hutchinson & Co., Ltd., 1958.

INDEX

Dan Costa

A fin whale at the surface.